The Reminiscences Of
Admiral Merlin O'Neill
U.S. Coast Guard (Retired)

Interviewed By
Peter Spectre

U.S. Naval Institute • Annapolis, Maryland

Copyright © 2004

Preface

The memoir that follows provides a march back through time—to the first half of the 20th century. Admiral O'Neill's career began with his entrance into the Coast Guard Academy during World War I. Several of the cutters during his early sea service were built in the 19th century. In these recollections he tells of Bering Sea patrols in the far North, patrolling against rumrunners during Prohibition, commanding a Navy attack transport during amphibious assaults in World War II, and eventually leading the service as a whole. He was Assistant Commandant from 1946 to 1949 and Commandant of the Coast Guard from 1950 to 1954. His leadership helped preserve the character of the service when government officials contemplated dismembering it in the early 1950s. Through his words Admiral O'Neill comes across as unassuming, a man who consistently put the interests of the service above his own ego.

This oral history represents a long-lost treasure. In the early 1970s Peter Spectre did the interviews at a time when the Naval Institute's oral history program was in its infancy. He was then an assistant editor in the Naval Institute's book department and a lieutenant (junior grade) in the Coast Guard Reserve. Even though the interviews were conducted and transcribed many years ago, for some reason the project was never completed until now. The transcript turned up in a recent inventory of unfinished material. I have converted it to digital format, added footnotes to provide additional background material, and done some very slight editing in the interests of smoothness and clarity. In large part, this transcript consists of the spoken words from Admiral O'Neill.

Welcome financial sponsorship for the completion of the project came from the Foundation for Coast Guard History, which was established "to promote the recognition and prestige of the United States Coast Guard by emphasizing its illustrious past." Captain Fred Herzberg is the foundation's executive director, and Vice Admiral Howard Thorsen is chairman of the board. They were instrumental in arranging a contribution to ensure that Admiral O'Neill's recollections will be made available for the benefit of history.

Finally, the Naval Institute expresses its gratitude to the Tawani Foundation and the Pritzker Military Library for their generous financial support of the oral history program that produced this memoir.

Paul Stillwell
Director, History Division
U.S. Naval Institute
December 2004

ADMIRAL MERLIN O'NEILL

UNITED STATES COAST GUARD (RETIRED)

Merlin O'Neill was born on 30 October 1898 in North Kenova, Ohio. After graduating from Morgan City High School, Morgan City, Louisiana he attended Western Kentucky State Normal School in 1916 and 1917, followed by a term at the U.S. Military Academy, West Point, New York. He then prepared service academy entrance examinations at Marion Institute, Marion, Alabama. He entered the U.S. Coast Guard Academy, New London, Connecticut, with an appointment as cadet in July 1918.

Graduating with an ensign's commission in March 1921, he subsequently advanced as follows: lieutenant (junior grade), 14 November 1921; lieutenant, 10 September 1925; lieutenant commander, 7 March 1929; commander, 25 May 1940; commander, 10 December 1942; captain, 1 June 1945; rear admiral, 1 February 1946; vice admiral, 1 January 1950; retired 1 June 1954 with rank of admiral.

His first assignment was on board USCGC *Gresham*, based at New York City. During following tours of duty on board USCGC *Haida* (April 1922 to December 1923) and USCGC *Algonquin* (in 1924), he made three long Bering Sea Patrol cruises with those vessels—two with the former and one with the latter.

After returning to the Atlantic Coast on board USCGC *Mojave*, O'Neill was detailed to the Philadelphia Navy Yard. His assignment was connected to the conversion of the former Navy destroyer *Ericsson* to Coast Guard duty for the suppression of smuggling. He served first as the executive officer of the destroyer after she was commissioned in May 1925. He became the commanding officer in 1927.

In September 1927 he was assigned to the Coast Guard Academy staff as an instructor. He acquired additional duties in November 1929, when he was appointed commandant of cadets. He made three summer practice cruises with the cadets during that period.

Between October 1930 and June 1933 he commanded the destroyers *Monaghan*, *Herndon*, and *Cassin*, respectively, on anti-smuggling operations along the North Atlantic Coast. During the next two and half years, he commanded USCGC *Apache*.

He was next stationed at Coast Guard Headquarters, Washington, D.C., from October 1935 to October 1942. During that time he served in the office of Operations and was also a Technical Adviser to the United States Delegation at the International Whaling Conference in London (May-June 1937). He became the first Chief Director of the Coast Guard Auxiliary (initially known as the Coast Guard Reserve), when that organization was formed in 1939.

During World War II he commanded the Coast Guard-manned attack troop transport USS *Leonard Wood* (APA-12) in the invasions at North Africa, Sicily, Gilbert Islands, and Marshall Islands. He was awarded the Legion of Merit for exceptionally meritorious conduct in the performance of outstanding services in the Sicily campaign and the Navy Unit Commendation for the transport's "exceptionally meritorious service in action against enemy aircraft, shore batteries, mines, and submarines."

In July 1944 Admiral O'Neill became commanding officer of the Coast Guard Amphibious Training Unit at Camp Lejeune, New River, North Carolina. A month later he was assigned as commander of the Baltimore Section of the Fifth Coast Guard District. His duties embraced the captain-of-the-port functions, the marine inspection office, pilot stations, a Coast Guard Base, a sub-recruiting station, and a training station at Fort McHenry.

Early in 1945 he was assigned as Assistant Chief, Finance and Supply Division, at Coast Guard Headquarters. Later that year, he was promoted to commodore and stationed at Norfolk, Virginia, as Commander Fifth Coast Guard District.

By nomination of President Harry S. Truman and with the confirmation of the Senate, O'Neill was appointed Assistant Commandant of the U.S. Coast Guard with rank of rear admiral as of 1 February 1946. He held this post until the Commandant, Admiral Joseph F. Farley, retired on 31 December 1949. O'Neill succeeded to the post of Commandant on 1 January 1950 with the rank of vice admiral. (His nomination as Commandant was announced by President Truman on 12 October 1949 and was confirmed by the Senate on 14 October 1949.)

When O'Neill took over as Commandant, the service had not changed much since its postwar demobilization. With a strength of just under 23,000 men, the service manned 177 cutters and 429 lighthouses in addition to various other craft and stations. Though no cutters served in combat operations, there would be considerable expansion as a result of the breakout of the Korean War in June 1950. President Truman's executive order subsequent to the Magnuson Act saw the Coast Guard become responsible for the execution of a national port security program. In performance of these duties the Coast Guard was to ferret out left-wing subversives in the nation's merchant fleet. The subsequent heavy-handed investigations led to the service's greatest levels of unpopularity since Prohibition.

Due to the fact that the Coast Guard Reserve had lapsed in the years following demobilization, the Korean War spurred the appropriation of funds to build an effective Coast Guard Reserve capable of supporting the service's wartime missions. The emergence of the Cold War saw Coast Guard personnel man the oceangoing radio station *Courier*. This vessel transmitted Voice of America broadcasts from the Greek island of Rhodes.

Though short of the statutory retirement age, O'Neill retired from the Coast Guard effective 1 June 1954 with the rank of full admiral. Under his leadership the Coast Guard's peacetime strength had reached its highest levels. At the time of his retirement, military personnel numbered just over 29,000 and this was supported by a civilian work force of just under 5,000. Though it may be said that O'Neill's tenure as Commandant was relatively unspectacular in comparison to others, it should also be noted that he did provide steady, competent leadership during a period of peacetime expansion.

Authorization

The U.S. Naval Institute is hereby authorized to make available to individuals, libraries, and other repositories of its choosing the transcripts of four oral history interviews concerning the life and career of the late Admiral Merlin O'Neill, U.S. Coast Guard (Retired). The four interviews were conducted on 31 January, 4 and 25 April 1970, and 7 March 1971 in collaboration with Peter H. Spectre for the U.S. Naval Institute.

Acting on behalf of the estate of the late Admiral O'Neill, the undersigned does hereby release and assign to the U.S. Naval Institute all right, title, restriction, and interest in the four interviews. The copyright in both the oral and transcribed versions shall be the sole property of the U.S. Naval Institute. The tape recordings of the interviews are and will remain the property of the U.S. Naval Institute.

Signed and sealed this 11th day of July 1985.

Esther T. O'Neill
(Mrs. Merlin O'Neill)

Interview Number 1 with Admiral Merlin O'Neill, U.S. Coast Guard (Retired)
Place: Admiral O'Neill's home in Lusby, Maryland
Date: Saturday, 31 January 1970
Interviewer: Peter Spectre

Peter Spectre: Admiral, I wonder if you could tell me a little bit about your childhood: where you were born, the day you were born, a little background for our interview.

Admiral O'Neill: Very well. I was born in North Kenova, Ohio, the 30th of October 1898. While I was a very young child, my parents moved to Delta, Ohio, which is at the southern tip of the state, down on the Ohio River. It is also next door to a small village known as South Point, meaning the southernmost post of the state. We lived there until I was 15 years old.

Peter Spectre: Is that a very rural area, or is it near a city?

Admiral O'Neill: It was a rural area, and my father was the country doctor of the horse-and-buggy variety. And I well remember Delta, Ohio. I went to school there. My first paying job was janitor of a two-room schoolhouse in Delta. I was in my early teens. Also, we lived right on the Ohio River, and there I was the proud owner of a rowboat, which in those days and in that section of the country were called johnboats. Then, when I was about 15 years old, my family moved to Morgan City, Louisiana. I went to high school there. I attended high school for three years, and while I was there I worked during the summer. I operated a small boat, about 26 feet long, working for one of the sugar plantation owners.

Peter Spectre: How did you get that job?

Admiral O'Neill: My father had the boat built to take care of some of his practice in the bayous in Louisiana. Then this plantation owner, who was my Sunday school teacher, asked me if I could transport him and some of his workmen around the bayous of his plantation on Avoca Island. That's right near the Atchafalaya River. It was there, this little city known as Morgan City, Louisiana, where I first learned about the Coast Guard. At that time it was known as the Revenue Cutter Service.* A revenue cutter came in and anchored just below the Southern Pacific Railroad bridge there. They came in apparently for boarding purposes, boarding and checking on boats and so forth, the usual work, making sure they had the proper papers and equipment.

Then, after I graduated from high school, the principal of the high school strongly recommended that I take up teaching as a profession. He was a graduate of the Western Kentucky State Normal School at Bowling Green, Kentucky. And so I entered there, and while I was there a friend of mine in Morgan City told me that he could get me an appointment to West Point as a second alternate—in other words, the number-three candidate.

Peter Spectre: How long was that after you started normal school?†

Admiral O'Neill: That was when I first entered normal school. And I was told that I could have an appointment as a second alternate, which would be for the following year. That was in 1916, and this appointment was for 1917. But he told me that the principal, the number-one man, and the first alternate—either one or the other—would get the appointment, and he would make my appointment the principal for the following year. I said that was agreeable with me, so I went on with my work there at the normal school.

Peter Spectre: How were your grades during high school and normal school?

Admiral O'Neill: Well, they were average for that type of school. You see, the high school down there at that time did not have what you call advanced courses. School in those days would correspond with junior high school nowadays, I would imagine. Well, anyway, it so turned out that the principal and first alternate for West Point both failed

---

* The U.S. Coast Guard was officially established on 28 January 1915 through the merger of the Revenue Cutter Service with the Life-Saving Service.
† A normal school was a preparatory college for aspiring schoolteachers; it was usually two years in duration.

their physical exams, and I received a letter stating that I had passed my physical exam, and I could have the appointment. Well, I talked it over with some of my friends, and they said, "Well, why don't you go ahead and try it?" So I did. I went to West Point in June of 1917.

Peter Spectre: What was your feeling about West Point and the Army and so forth in light of your later career?

Admiral O'Neill: I had no particular desire to go to West Point, because I had never had any connection with the Army, or the Navy, for that matter. I had with what was known as the Revenue Cutter Service, because it was stationed on the Ohio River. Well, anyway, I went on to West Point in June 1917, and I realized shortly after I got there that I was not prepared for service in any of the military academies with the amount of schooling that I had had. So, while I was there, one day I saw in the *Army-Navy Journal*—I think that magazine might be out of print nowadays—but in the *Army-Navy Journal* there was a notice of a competitive exam for the Coast Guard Academy.

Peter Spectre: What was your weakest point at West Point?

Admiral O'Neill: Mathematics. Then that rang a bell with me. The notice said that there would be a competitive exam to be held in May or June of 1918 and listed the various cities in the United States where the exam would be held. That rang a bell with me, and remembering that I, as I say, was not prepared at that time for any college—military or otherwise—I resigned in January 1918 and immediately enrolled at the Marion Military Institute at Marion, Alabama.

Peter Spectre: How did you hear of that school?

Admiral O'Neill: They also had an ad in the *Army-Navy Journal* stating that they had a preparatory course for young men who were preparing for Annapolis, West Point, and the Coast Guard Academy. That's how I happened to know about Marion Institute.

Peter Spectre: How did your parents feel about you resigning from West Point?

Admiral O'Neill: I talked it over with them and convinced them I wasn't prepared. I wasn't particularly interested in it, but I did want to try for the Coast Guard Academy. So they went along with me on the idea of going to Marion and taking this prep course. That prep course was actually 98% mathematics; that's what it was. And there were quite a few young men there prepping for the three military academies, and a number preparing for the Coast Guard Academy. My roommate there at prep school passed the exam, and he was my roommate at the Coast Guard Academy for one year. Well, anyway, then in June I took the competitive exam for the Coast Guard and passed it and entered the Academy in July—I think it was the latter part of July—1918 and went through the usual courses there. It was my good fortune to graduate number one in the class.

Peter Spectre: Could you tell me a little bit about the Coast Guard Academy when you were there?

Admiral O'Neill: Well, it was small. It was a very much smaller institution than it is today. It was located at Fort Trumbull, New London, and some of our classrooms were in the old Civil War forts there. It was a typical fort of Civil War days, and our barracks were wooden structures that were built at the beginning of World War I. We took over some of them for the Academy and the cadets. When I entered there, there were only a total of 52 cadets.

Peter Spectre: In all four classes?

Admiral O'Neill: Well, there were only three classes.

Peter Spectre: It was a three-year course?

Admiral O'Neill: It was a three-year course. It was shortened to two and a half years on account of World War I. We graduated in two and a half years instead of three years. But when I entered there were 52 cadets, and I was number 51, because one reported a week after I did, so I wasn't exactly low man on the totem pole.

Peter Spectre: How many were in your class?

Admiral O'Neill: We were 15, and only 4 graduated.

Peter Spectre: What happened to the other 11?

Admiral O'Neill: Well, some failed, but a majority resigned, because they weren't interested in the Coast Guard as a career. And there may have been a few who wanted to avoid the man in the brown suit, as we say. I don't know for sure, but I suspect that that was the case.

Peter Spectre: What course of instruction did you pursue? Were you an engineer student, or did you have a distinction?

Admiral O'Neill: Well, we had a distinction. We had line cadets and engineer cadets in those days. The engineer cadets—that was a one-year course. Mine was the line. That was for seamanship, and radio, and electricity, and subjects of that nature.

Peter Spectre: When you arrived there, were you assigned to one or the other, or did you have a choice?

Admiral O'Neill: I had to go in as line, because in order to go in as engineer you had to be a graduate of an engineering school.

Peter Spectre: You had to have been to college then?

Admiral O'Neill: Yes.

Peter Spectre: So that actually the engineering students were similar to what we have in OCS now?[*]

Admiral O'Neill: That's right. Indoctrination primarily. Acquaint them with the service etiquette, and customs and routine, and a smattering of seamanship.

Peter Spectre: Who were your instructors? Were they Coast Guardsmen, or were they civilians?

Admiral O'Neill: We had one civilian; our mathematics instructor was a civilian. All the rest were commissioned officers.

Peter Spectre: How were they? Were they good instructors?

Admiral O'Neill: Excellent, excellent. Our French instructor had spent some time in France purposefully to prepare himself, and our engineering instructor was a regular engineering officer in the Coast Guard—all very able, competent men.

Peter Spectre: Were the commissioned instructors permanently assigned there?

Admiral O'Neill: No, no. They were assigned there for a tour, say, of three or four years. Now, the civilian mathematics instructor was there for life. He was one of the outstanding mathematicians in the country.

Peter Spectre: What was his name?

Admiral O'Neill: Professor Dimick.[†]

---

[*] OCS – Officer Candidate School.
[†] Professor Chester E. Dimick.

Peter Spectre: You had your classroom instruction. What other kind of practical training did you have?

Admiral O'Neill: Well, during the summer we had the summer cruises for practical seamanship and navigation. In the wintertime, of course, it was theoretical, practically all of it. But aboard the training ships we usually made about a two or two-and-a-half-months cruise, where we alternated in engine room duty and fireroom duty and various watch-standing duties like lookouts and wheelman, and also junior officer of the deck for officer of the deck training, so someday if we were to be commissioned—

Peter Spectre: Did the Coast Guard Academy have their own training ships at that time, or did you train on regular Coast Guard—?

Admiral O'Neill: No, they had their own training ships. When I first reported there, the training ship was a regular cutter, the *Onondaga* and assigned there for that purpose.[*] Then later on she was relieved by the *Itasca* that was formerly a Navy gunboat.[†] Then later on, after I graduated, she was relieved by the *Alexander Hamilton* as a training ship.[‡]

Peter Spectre: Did you train in sail at all?

Admiral O'Neill: Yes, the *Itasca* carried sails. We never really sailed a ship. We would put up the sails but only temporarily, just for the training. But we wouldn't shut down the engines and just sail alone. Sometimes we used staysails in stormy weather and, of course, furled the sails for practice and to learn the terminology—which we never used after we graduated.

---

[*] The 205-foot-long, 1,181-ton *Onondaga* was commissioned 24 October 1898, served in World War I, and was decommissioned 5 November 1919

[†] The 188-foot, 839-ton USS *Bancroft* was built for the Navy as a training vessel and gunboat; she was commissioned by the Navy on 3 March 1893. She was transferred to the Revenue Cutter Service 30 June 1906 and renamed *Itasca*. She was eventually sold by the Coast Guard on 11 May 1922.

[‡] The 204-foot, 1,010-ton USS *Vicksburg* was commissioned as a Navy gunboat on 23 October 1897. On 2 May 1921 she was transferred to the Coast Guard and on 18 August 1922 renamed *Alexander Hamilton*. She served as a Coast Guard Academy training ship until 1930.

Peter Spectre: Where did you go on your cruises?

Admiral O'Neill: Well, the first year, that was '18, the war was still on. We just cruised along the eastern seacoast: around Long Island Sound, up off the New England coast, down off the eastern coast down as far as the Carolinas. And then the following year we made a cruise to the Caribbean, down through the Panama Canal. Then, the third summer I was there, on a training ship we made a trip to Europe. We went to England, France, and the Azore Islands, then back to New London. Then I graduated from there in 1921, and I was assigned to a cutter in New York for one year. Then I was transferred to a cutter that was stationed in Seattle, Washington.

Peter Spectre: What was the name of the cutter on your first assignment in New York?

Admiral O'Neill: The *Gresham*.[*]

Peter Spectre: Did you have any choice in your assignment?

Admiral O'Neill: No.

Peter Spectre: None at all?

Admiral O'Neill: Not at all, never.

Peter Spectre: Were you happy with your assignment?

Admiral O'Neill: Oh, yes. I was very fortunate; I had good assignments all through my career.

---

[*] The 206-foot, 1,090 cutter *Gresham* was commissioned 30 May 1897 and served in World War I. She was decommissioned in 1935, later brought back for brief service in World War II.

Peter Spectre: Could I ask you a little bit about what your first duties were on the *Gresham*?

Admiral O'Neill: Oh, I was junior officer of the deck with related duties. I was the clothing officer, and I had one of the divisions aboard to teach the men signaling and duties of that kind. We used to have our drills—man-overboard drills, fire drills, collision drills—and I was responsible for that particular division of men that I had as the junior officer.

Peter Spectre: How many officers were there on board?

Admiral O'Neill: There were only two regular watch officers. Another youngster that graduated ahead of me was the other one. Then there was the executive officer. He didn't stand watches except when we were under way at sea, and then the commanding officer and the engineering officer.

Peter Spectre: How big was the *Gresham*?

Admiral O'Neill: She was 250 feet.

Peter Spectre: What type of duty did the *Gresham* engage in?

Admiral O'Neill: Well, it was regular Coast Guard duty in those days. It was search and rescue primarily, and boarding duties—you know, to check on equipment of boats and ships and tugs in Baltimore Harbor. We had to do a great deal of small-boat boarding with ships, boats, tugs and barges, ferryboats, and things like that. We had to cruise over our station; our station was from Block Island to Cape May. That was the area of the ocean we were responsible for, the ship was responsible for.

Peter Spectre: Were there any other Coast Guard cutters that covered that area?

Admiral O'Neill: No, there were two harbor tugs used to carry Customs men, but we were the only Coast Guard seagoing ship there.

Peter Spectre: So that when you weren't cruising, when you were on the shore base, there was no one on the station as the Coast Guard?

Admiral O'Neill: No, it wasn't a constant patrol at sea, no. But, you see, we anchored there. We had no base; we had to anchor or stay at Staten Island. That was our regular anchorage, and we could get out to sea very easily, just down the channel there. But our orders were in those days to cruise over the station at least once a month. That could take several days to cruise if there were no calls, but we were constantly ready to go night or day and many times went out late at night.

Peter Spectre: Did you live on board ship?

Admiral O'Neill: Oh, yes; oh, yes.

Peter Spectre: Or did you live in New York?

Admiral O'Neill: No, I lived on board.

Peter Spectre: When did you meet your wife?

Admiral O'Neill: While I was a cadet at New London.

Peter Spectre: When did you marry her?

Admiral O'Neill: We were married in 1925 when I came back from the Bering Sea duty.

Peter Spectre: Was your wife a student at Connecticut College for Women?

Admiral O'Neill: No, no, she was in high school in New London when I met her, and we became engaged before I left the Academy. Then the fact that I was going to be transferred from the place for a while, we waited until I got settled down a little bit nearer on the East Coast.

Peter Spectre: She originally came from New England?

Admiral O'Neill: She's a New London girl.

Peter Spectre: Was there any exciting activity while you were on the *Gresham*? Anything out of the ordinary?

Admiral O'Neill: No, I don't recall any. It was rather quiet in those days; there was no smuggling or anything like that. It was routine search-and-rescue work.

Peter Spectre: We could go on to your next station.

Admiral O'Neill: Well, let's see. I was transferred to the cutter *Haida* at Seattle, Washington.[*]

Peter Spectre: Was this an involuntary assignment? Did you request the change?

Admiral O'Neill: No, I was just ordered there.

Peter Spectre: Did the training that you received at the Coast Guard Academy live up to your expectations or the service's expectations when you got your first assignment and second assignment? Do you think you were well trained or well prepared for the duty that you were assigned to?

---

[*] USCGC *Haida* (WPG-45) was a member of the *Tampa* class, the first in the service with turbo-electric drive and the largest and most advanced cutters of the time. The 240-foot, 1,506-ton *Haida* was commissioned on 26 October 1921, served through World War II, and was decommissioned in 1947.

Admiral O'Neill: Oh, I felt so, and I think others felt so, too, because when I graduated from the Academy in early March I didn't get my commission immediately. It took a while for them to go through, so I was sent down to the *Gresham* in New York as a cadet. I was a graduate of the Academy, but my rank was still cadet. The commanding officer apparently felt safe enough to let me take a bridge watch at sea as a cadet. And I felt competent to do so because of our training at the Academy, which I felt was excellent. You see, there was just a small load of us, and I think—and still feel—that having just a few like that, we rotated frequently, and we had more opportunity, more practice, so to speak, in the various duties that we were assigned to for training.

Peter Spectre: I see. How did you get along with the enlisted men on your ship?

Admiral O'Neill: Oh, fine, very well.

Peter Spectre: What about the other three men that graduated with you at that time? Did they have any trouble adjusting to the service?

Admiral O'Neill: No, none at all. They were transferred to other ships. I forget now where.

Peter Spectre: Did you keep in touch with them?

Admiral O'Neill: Oh, yes, yes. There's only one living now. He retired at the end of World War II.

Peter Spectre: What's his name?

Admiral O'Neill: N. R. Stiles.[*] He was the assistant personnel officer at Coast Guard Headquarters during World War II.

---

[*] Captain Norman R. Stiles, USCG, retired from active duty on 1 April 1946. He died 16 June 1973.

Peter Spectre: What type of duty was the *Haida* on?

Admiral O'Neill: Well, it was during the summer. The cruises then usually went up in the spring and came down in the late fall—up in the Bering Sea area and North Pacific, a seven months' cruise. We used to leave about the middle of April and come back in the latter part of November. All that time was spent around the Pribilof Islands on regular Coast Guard duty and also enforcing that sealing convention. It was a convention signed by the United States and Japan and Russia to prevent pelagic sealing, that is, the killing of female seals at sea, where they go offshore for food, leaving their young on the rookery. We had that duty.

Peter Spectre: Were there other ships from Japan and Russia involved in this patrol?

Admiral O'Neill: Not in our area. They were over in their areas but not around the Pribilof Islands and the Bering Sea.

Peter Spectre: So, according to the convention, each country had its own area. Were there any other Coast Guard cutters that did this with you? In other words, when you went out to the station, did someone else take your place?

Admiral O'Neill: No. The only other cutter during those years that came up there while we were there—we were there three years—was the old cutter *Bear*.[*] They came through there; they weren't involved in that kind of seal patrol work, as we called it. They usually went up as far as Point Barrow, and they, as well as ourselves, carried a doctor and a dentist to treat the natives. The dentist would treat them for their dental troubles wherever we went in the native villages, and the doctor would go ashore with his pharmacist's mate and make sick calls on the natives.[†]

---

[*] The *Bear* was a famous old cutter, built in 1873 in Scotland. In 1885 she began a long period of service as a Revenue Marine cutter; she often served in the Arctic. She was decommissioned by the Coast Guard on 3 May 1929 and later served as a museum ship and as a U.S. Navy ship.
[†] Pharmacist's mate was an enlisted rating for an individual who specialized in the medical area.

Peter Spectre: You hear a lot about the Coast Guard being more or less the long arm of the government in Alaska during this period of time. How true is that?

Admiral O'Neill: Well, that captain was told he was the United States commissioner. He was so appointed. He could hold court, perform marriages, had tremendous authority. Also, the executive officer was a United States marshal, so appointed. He could make arrests. I think that's where that probably came into usage, that expression "long arm."

Peter Spectre: Did you perform more or less the way a circuit judge performs? Did you have a regular schedule where you arrived at certain ports at scheduled times so that a problem in the area could be solved at that time?

Admiral O'Neill: Yes, to some extent. It was a circuit-riding operation, but we didn't have to be there at an exact date. We would go in, you see, and maybe stay there for several days till they rounded up the culprits, if any, and if there was no preacher ashore, then the captain would perform a few marriages and things like that. But, in addition to that, as I say, we had regular Coast Guard duties, such as rescue. There wasn't much of that, because there was very little shipping up there, very little boating.

There was a mail boat that came up once a month into that area in those days. There was a combination freight and passenger ship that ran out of Seattle, the *Victoria*. They would make one trip a summer, and that's all. The rest of the time we were cruising. We cruised out as far as Attu Island—that's the westernmost tip of the Aleutian chain—and then up into the Bristol Bay, up as far as Nome, down around the Alaska peninsula, Kodiak Island and that area through there. That's the North Pacific.

Peter Spectre: As you list off these names—and they're very exciting-sounding places; I don't know if you'd call them exotic—but what was it like being there? Did you enjoy it?

Admiral O'Neill: Do you mean the duty?

Peter Spectre: Yes, and going to these various places like Attu and Bristol Bay and Nome. These are all places that people hear about very romantic things happening there, very exciting things.

Admiral O'Neill: Well, it was probably the most interesting service that I had. Of course, I was a junior officer. I had to stand my watches, but I had plenty of leisure time. I could go ashore. We sometimes went ashore, several of us. On that ship there were more officers than on my first assignment, so we weren't tied down quite as much. At, for example, Attu Island, there was a native village there, Aleuts, and they lived by fishing and by killing foxes and selling the fox skins to traders that would come through in small schooners. And the women were famous for weaving baskets. I have an Attu basket here that I'll show you in a minute. They're museum pieces now, because all the natives in the village of Attu were captured by the Japs at the beginning of World War II, when Japan captured the island, and they hauled them off to Japan. At that time I think there were about 70 or 80 natives in the village. It was that number when I was up there, and I think most of them died in captivity. That's the way I heard—read about it somewhere.

Then another interesting part of that Bering Sea patrol—by the way, it is now called the Alaskan patrol; those days it was the Bering Sea patrol. Up in Bristol Bay, where there are a number of salmon canneries, we used to enjoy going ashore and watching the canning of the salmon, bringing the fish in in their boats, their lighters. That was interesting. Then around Nome it was sort of an arctic village in those days. I understand it's more or less of a big city now.

Peter Spectre: Most of those places have really grown.

Admiral O'Neill: Yes. So we used to enjoy going ashore and talking to the old sourdoughs, as they called them, and some of the old miners that were still there.

Peter Spectre: Were you well received by the people?

Admiral O'Neill: Oh, my, yes.

Peter Spectre: Nowadays when the law shows up, nobody's happy.

Admiral O'Neill: They waved their hats when we came to town, as the expression goes. No, they were glad, because, as I say, we would haul mail on those islands out there. There were a number of inhabited islands to the westward there; I just cited Attu as an example. And there were so few white people that Unalaska, where we based, across from the little bay there was a place called Dutch Harbor, where we took aboard our oil. There were some oil tanks there that were run by the Alaska Commercial Company in those days. There were about half a dozen white people in Unalaska and about 100 Aleuts. There was a schoolteacher and his wife, a trader and his wife, the manager of the Alaska Commercial Company, and a man who ran the fuel operation—about six, maybe eight white people there. But we tied up to a pier there, so we were right in town, so to speak.

Peter Spectre: You got your oil in Unalaska. How did you get your regular supplies, other than fuel?

Admiral O'Neill: Well, we would get some supplies from this one ship that came up, the *Victoria*, but we had to carry all of our supplies from Seattle. We would run out of fresh vegetables, produce, which we missed very much, like lettuce and carrots and celery and things like that. We could get some of that from this one ship, as I say, but everything else came out of a tin can.

I remember one thing. When I was commissary officer of the *Haida* we had to go down in the hold of the ship about every two or three weeks and turn the cases of eggs over. The eggs were not under refrigeration. You had to turn them over so that the yolk did not adhere to the shell from sitting in one place all the time. By the end of the season, one of the Filipino cooks aboard would say, "No can poach; can scramble." That's just a sidelight and all, but most everything came in a tin can. We'd get a little honey for fresh stores and lots of fishing. We carried seines, and we could seine there for salmon and halibut, and there were other kinds of edible fish that we would haul in by the boatload when we were in port somewhere. The crew always got a big kick out of that. It was an all-hands affair. It was fish for everybody, and they used to come along and get a big kick out of it, especially when we would haul in some young octopus. For the Filipino boys aboard the boat, the cooks in the mess room, some parts of the octopus they considered a rare delicacy. Nobody else paid any attention to it.

Peter Spectre: Did you carry any supplies to the villages that you visited?

Admiral O'Neill: No.

Peter Spectre: Just mail?

Admiral O'Neill: No. Just mail and medical attention.

Peter Spectre: What kind of ship was the *Haida*?

Admiral O'Neill: She was a 255-foot cutter, a pretty good cutter.

Peter Spectre: Was it built especially for the Coast Guard?

Admiral O'Neill: Yes. There were seven or eight of that class built on the West Coast, and I made two cruises on the *Haida* and one cruise on another one, the *Algonquin*.*

Peter Spectre: This was on the Bering Sea patrol?

Admiral O'Neill: Bering Sea patrol. On the *Algonquin*, that was in 1924. That was the year that the Army around-the-world fliers took off to fly around the world in four of

---

* The *Algonquin* was a sister ship of the *Onondaga*, which had been a training ship during O'Neill's time as a Coast Guard Academy cadet. The *Algonquin* was commissioned 20 June 1898 and eventually decommissioned 11 December 1930 and sold.

those Douglas planes.[*] There were two or three cutters assigned up there then, and our job was to help them as far as logistics was concerned. We carried a spare engine aboard, and one of the planes flown by Major Martin landed there on the Alaska Peninsula in a place called Portage Bay. He had engine trouble, a forced landing. We were sent over to help him take the engine out and put the new one in. I think those were Packard engines; I'm not sure.

Anyway, we anchored right at the mouth of the bay, and our engineers' force installed this engine for him. He had a mechanic with him, but one man couldn't do it. It was our crew and our engineers that did the work. So they got the new engine installed, tried it out, and it worked fine, so he took off the following morning in a snowstorm to go to westward to Unalaska to meet the other three fliers who were waiting for him in Unalaska. Well, he disappeared. So then we were all turned to searching the shoreline to try to find him. Well, he finally showed up. He and his mechanic had crashed on a small hill in the interior of the Alaska Peninsula.[†] They had walked the rest of the way over to the northern side of the Alaska Peninsula, where they went into a cannery station there that had a radio. The radio announced that they had shown up and were in good health. So one of the ships went up there and picked them up. So that, as the saying goes today, scrubbed their efforts for the around-the-world flight, and the other three took off without them.

Peter Spectre: They had more than one plane on this—

Admiral O'Neill: There were four planes involved. They were the Douglas biplanes, single engine. That was the highlight of our 1924 cruise.

Peter Spectre: The cutters that you were on, the *Algonquin* and the *Haida*, were they equipped for work in the ice?

---

[*] Major Frederick L. Martin, U.S. Army Air Service, commanded the first-ever around-the-world airplane flight. Four single-engine biplanes, based on the design of the Douglas DT-2 torpedo bomber, began the flight. The planes left Sand Point, near Seattle, on 6 April 1924. One crashed into a mountain near Dutch Harbor, Alaska, and one was left to sink in the Atlantic Ocean. Two of the planes completed the east-to-west flight, which wound up in Seattle on 28 September. They covered some 26,000 miles in 175 days.
[†] The crash was on 30 April 1924.

Admiral O'Neill: No, no.

Peter Spectre: Did you encounter ice?

Admiral O'Neill: Well, we encountered ice when we'd go up as far as Nome and Cape Prince of Wales, up there, but it was floe ice, and we could dodge it. I mean, it was just floating, chunks of ice that we could dodge around and get away from.

Peter Spectre: The hull wasn't specially rigged for icebreaking?

Admiral O'Neill: No, no, they were not icebreakers. They came later.

Peter Spectre: You say our patrols lasted for seven or nine months?

Admiral O'Neill: Well, the first patrol was seven months; the second patrol was six months; and the third patrol I made was five.

Peter Spectre: It was steadily decreased.

Admiral O'Neill: Yes, decreasing. I don't know what the lengths of their patrols are now. They still maintain a patrol up there, but we have ships and planes now at Kodiak, which is right there next door. One interesting thing about the Bering Sea patrol back in those days were those beautiful square-rigged ships—the cannery fleet, as they were called. And they were also referred to as the Star boats. They were all based around California, principally around Oakland.

Peter Spectre: Why were they called Star boats?

Admiral O'Neill: Because their names were *Star of India*, *Star of Scotland*, *Star of Finland*. I mention those just to give you an example. Then there were a few that did not carry the Star designation. But there was quite a fleet of them, and we used to stand by at Unimak Pass—that's the opening between the tip end of the Alaska Peninsula and the first of the Aleutian Islands to the west. They had to go through there. They had to have favorable weather. They had no power. They had to have a favorable wind, and so they would jockey around and sail around south of Unimak Pass and wait for the time, the tide, and the wind, and weather; then they'd go through there.

The pass was wide—maybe six or eight miles wide—so they had plenty of room. But it was a beautiful sight to see them sailing around, just waiting until the time. Then they'd go up into Bristol Bay and anchor off the canneries. They carried the cannery crews around, Chinese and Mexicans. The actual complement of those ships was surprisingly low. Usually the complement was about 30 or 35 in the crew, and that was all. But they would carry 300 or 400 so-called passengers as cannery workers. Then at the end of the cannery season they would load the canned salmon aboard these ships and sail them back down to San Francisco.

Peter Spectre: So they only made one voyage a year?

Admiral O'Neill: They'd go up there every spring, and while they were going through the pass there, sometimes it would take two or three weeks for them all to get through. We had to stand by there so that if any of them got into trouble we would help them. In other words, if you got onto a lee shore and couldn't claw off, as they call it—it means, as they say, clawing off the lee shore, we would go alongside and put a line on him and haul him out to clear water.

Peter Spectre: Did you ever have any casualties or disasters among—?

Admiral O'Neill: No, no. Most unusual, but nothing happened in the three years I was up there.

Peter Spectre: What did you do in those months that you weren't on patrol? You were back in Seattle?

Admiral O'Neill: Well, a good part of the time was overhaul, getting ready to go next spring, and also standing by in case of an SOS call. If we weren't completely disabled with engines taken apart, we would get under way and go out and answer the call. We did that several times.

Peter Spectre: Was that when you took your leave?

Admiral O'Neill: We'd take leave, and, as I say, a good part of it was overhaul. You see, we weren't able to do much work aboard ship, like painting and chipping and all up there; it was just too cold. It wasn't down around 20 degrees below zero or anything like that, but it was damp all the time, foggy and a cold breeze blowing most of the time. No snow on the ground. Snow on the mountain peaks but nothing on the ground.

Peter Spectre: What about sealers? Was it much work patrolling these sealing grounds? Did you encounter poachers during this period of time?

Admiral O'Neill: No, we did not. We cruised there most all the time. There was a second cutter that was sent up to alternate with us on some of our patrols—I forget the name of it now—and the only arrest that I recall being made in both seas, it was an Aleut aboard a small boat. He had taken a sea otter. But it was interesting around the Pribilof Islands, around the rookeries. The Department of Bureau Fisheries had crews on St. Paul and St. George islands, where they killed the fur seals, the young bachelor fur seals, for the pelts. Back in those days the herd was small; I think the total population of the fur seals in the Pribilofs in those days was about 50,000. Then, later on, on account of the protection given them by the Coast Guard ships, the herd increased considerably.

Peter Spectre: Before that they were being—

Admiral O'Neill: Depleted and would have become extinct, because the poachers, as I said, were killing the mother seals out at sea, and then that would mean the pups would die.

Peter Spectre: At that period of time was this considered good duty?

Admiral O'Neill: Yes, it was.

Peter Spectre: Every year the Coast Guard or the Navy or the Army and so forth has its own duty that's considered good and duty that's considered bad, and it changes every decade.

Admiral O'Neill: Well, I'll qualify that a little bit. It was not considered desirable duty by some of the married men because of the separation from their families for that period of time. As far as the unmarried men were concerned, of which I was a member of the clan up to that time, we thought it was terrific because it was something to do all the time. There were no dull moments, as the saying goes.

Peter Spectre: I can imagine it would be. What happened to you then at the end of this?

Admiral O'Neill: Well, at the end of that I was transferred to the cutter *Mojave*, and that was in December of 1924.[*] We came around to the East Coast through the Panama Canal.

Peter Spectre: Where was the *Mojave* when you picked it up?

Admiral O'Neill: In Seattle, Washington. Then we came around through the Panama Canal and up to Philadelphia, where some of us were transferred to Navy destroyers that were based there, being outfitted for rum patrol.

---

[*] USCGC *Mojave*, a sister ship of the *Haida* in which O'Neill had served earlier, was commissioned 12 December 1921, served in World War II, and was eventually decommissioned 3 July 1947.

Peter Spectre: So that actually your period of time on the *Mojave* was really in transit from the West Coast?

Admiral O'Neill: That's right. I was aboard about a month, maybe six weeks; that's all. That was just working my way around to the East Coast. I was the navigator aboard the *Mojave* and worked around to Philadelphia.

Peter Spectre: Is the *Mojave* the ship that was built as a derelict destroyer? Do you know?

Admiral O'Neill: Well, most of the cutters back in those days were referred to as derelict destroyers.

Peter Spectre: Well, Captain Capron told me a while ago that there was a Coast Guard cutter that was built specifically for derelict destroyer, that they actually intended it to be that way, whereas the other ones had been converted, or their mission had been changed.[*] This one was specifically designed for it. I think he said the *Mojave*, but I can't remember exactly. He said that the stack was painted with striped bands around it. I think it was red and white stripes.

Admiral O'Neill: Well, that may be, but the *Mojave* wasn't so painted when I was aboard.

Peter Spectre: Maybe it was another ship then.

Admiral O'Neill: But we were all equipped to destroy derelicts. We carried TNT aboard, and, for example, if a schooner was sunk off the East Coast we blew up several of them when I was aboard the *Gresham*. We'd see sometimes just the top of the mast sticking up. They couldn't be salvaged, so what we would do, we would lower these charges of

---

[*] Spectre did the interviews for the Naval Institute oral history of Captain Walter C. Capron, USCG (Ret.).

TNT, sited on the mast, and then get away a distance in the boat, throw the switch, and blow the mast out. That was destroying a derelict, as far as passing ships were concerned, so they wouldn't get into trouble.

Peter Spectre: Isn't that sort of dangerous?

Admiral O'Neill: Oh, no, no, no. Nothing was connected until you'd get way off in your boat. You'd connect it, you see, and then you'd throw your switch, and there she goes. It would be dangerous if you didn't do that.

So then we arrived in Philadelphia. That was early January of 1925. Then I took leave and went up to New London, Connecticut, and married the young lady whom I had met while I was a cadet. We were married on the 25th of January, and we just celebrated our 45th wedding anniversary here last Saturday.

Peter Spectre: You got married because you realized you were going to be—

Admiral O'Neill: Yes, I was going to be stationed. See, the ship that I was assigned to, the destroyer, their homeport was to be New London, Connecticut. We knew we were going to go right back to her hometown.

Peter Spectre: Was this another involuntary assignment? In other words, did you ask for it?

Admiral O'Neill: No, no. I don't think any time in my service career I asked for an assignment or asked to be relieved of an assignment.

Peter Spectre: Was that the practice? I know now they give you a card to fill out, and you list your first three choices and your first three locations, and so forth. That wasn't the practice when you were—?

Admiral O'Neill: It was the practice to a limited extent. On the old-type fitness reports, there was a place there for your preference for duty. And there was an old saying in those days, sarcastically or facetiously, if you asked for a certain station the chances were 100 to 1 you'd never get it. You'd go to something else far removed from that.

Peter Spectre: So you put down someplace that you didn't want to go?

Admiral O'Neill: That was the idea. But I'm sure that I never asked for a station or to be relieved of a station. I enjoyed all of my service duties.

Peter Spectre: Tell me about the Navy destroyers, the background and so forth.

Admiral O'Neill: Of course, the rum war had started, and the biggest problem was to picket these supply ships that were bringing the liquor in from Nova Scotia and Canada to transfer it to the fast motorboats that were operating from ports on the East Coast.* The Navy had a large number of these World War I destroyers, decommissioned in what we called the back channel at the Philadelphia Navy Yard. I forget now—there were, oh, at least eight or ten being reconditioned to be back into service while I was there. I was assigned as the executive officer of the *Ericsson*.†

Peter Spectre: Did those destroyers keep their Navy names when they were put into Coast Guard service?

Admiral O'Neill: Yes, they kept their Navy names. So then after we were married, I came back to Philadelphia, and we lived there until May, when the ship was completed

---

* The 18th Amendment to the Constitution was ratified in 1919 and went into effect in 1920, prohibiting the consumption of alcoholic beverages in the United States. The Volstead Act, enacted by Congress in 1919, spelled out the penalties for violations. In December 1933 the ratification of the 21st Amendment repealed the 18th Amendment and thus ended national prohibition. The Coast Guard had the mission of preventing the importation of alcoholic beverages, analogous to its war against drugs in recent years.

† USS *Ericsson* (later DD-56), an *O'Brien*-class destroyer, was commissioned 14 August 1915. She had a standard displacement of 1,050 tons, was 305 feet long, and 31 feet in the beam. Her top speed was 29 knots. She was armed with four 4-inch guns, and 16 21-inch torpedo tubes. She was decommissioned by the Navy on 16 June 1922 at the Philadelphia Navy Yard and transferred to the Coast Guard on 7 June 1924. She was commissioned by the Coast Guard on 28 May 1925 with the new hull number of CG-5.

and put back in commission. Then we were based at New London. There were about ten other destroyers; we were in groups of five.

Peter Spectre: What kind of condition were they in?

Admiral O'Neill: Well, they were in very good condition. They'd been laid up well by the Navy, and, of course, they had all this red paint all over everything—this red lead, we called it—and they had anti-corrosive paint of various kinds.[*] The machinery had been laid up well, heavily greased. It took a long time, of course, to clean up everything, repaint the interior of the ship and the exterior of the ship. Some of the turbines had to be overhauled, and some of the pumps had to be overhauled, but, by and large, they were in surprisingly good shape. They didn't have that system of mothballing in those days that they have today with the battleships and cruisers and aircraft carriers—ships of that kind.

It was interesting duty for watch officers, especially COs and execs.[†] I called it fun handling them, because they had so much power. They were twin screws, and we could just spin them around. They were quite long, around 300 feet.

Peter Spectre: When you see pictures of them, they look like rails going through the water.

Admiral O'Neill: Yes.

Peter Spectre: Were they uncomfortable to sail on?

Admiral O'Neill: No, the quarters were small. The crew's quarters were in tiered bunks, of course, and a little bit cramped. The officers' staterooms were small, little, tiny rooms. You'd call them a clothes closet today, but they were comfortable. At sea they rode very well. Any ship will roll and pitch in a storm at sea; you can't avoid that. It was very interesting duty. Later on I was fortunate to have command of the *Ericsson* and also two

---

[*] Red lead is the nickname for an orange-colored anti-corrosive primer paint applied to bare metal before the regular paint is put on.
[†] CO – commanding officer.

or three of the other ships for short periods. Then after I was on that duty for three years—

Peter Spectre: Tell me a little bit about the operations that you were involved with.

Admiral O'Neill: Well, some were stationed in New York, some in New London, and some in Boston. Like you might say flotillas—divisions, we called them. I think there were five stationed in New York, ten in New London, and five in Boston—some number like that. We would relieve each other at sea, different parts of the coast. Most of the patrolling was south of Long Island and out around Nantucket, Martha's Vineyard Island, and then up east of Boston. Those were the principal areas.

Peter Spectre: Did each squadron or flotilla have a particular area, or did you just—?

Admiral O'Neill: No, we were assigned an area by the destroyer force commander. His headquarters were in New London, and we would sail, and we would be given certain areas to patrol. The idea was to patrol our area to see if we could find one of these mother ships—supply ships loaded with liquor. Well, if we found one, we would start picketing it, as we called it, in other words, prevent contact with a small fast motorboat from shore.

Well, that worked out all right except in foggy weather; then they would escape because there was no such thing as radar. If we had had radar then, that would have been very simple, but he would disappear because we couldn't find him. When the fog cleared, maybe the following day, the search would have to be started, and he might be many miles away. In that respect, it was not very effective. It did slow down maybe some of the transfer of liquor to the small boats, but I think very little. That was not the answer to the rum patrol problem. They finally solved it by passing an amendment.

Peter Spectre: I've heard that this period of time was great for the officers of the Coast Guard, because when they were playing cat and mouse with these rumrunners they had a chance to really engage in serious maneuvering in the ships and that this was an asset during the Second World War. Would you confirm?

Admiral O'Neill: Well, yes, I would. Another thing—you see, we would frequently cruise in formation in and out of harbors or maybe going south for target practice. Sometimes one division would be relieved for a month or six weeks to go south for target practice, and we'd cruise down in formation, in columns. Keeping station in columns came in handy in World War II on account of the convoy, where everything was tight formation and had to stay within 200 yards of the ship right ahead of you. That was true. And the ship handling was excellent practice. It came in handy, of course, later on. And then the signaling between ships—it was terrific training for all Coast Guard officers on that destroyer post duty when they were transferred to Navy ships in '41.

Peter Spectre: Were most of the offices in the East Coast during that time engaged in running protection duties?

Admiral O'Neill: A good majority, yes. Of course, while we were on this rum patrol we were also on search-and-rescue duty, too, and performed it quite a bit. If a ship was in distress, the destroyer would be relieved from that and sent out to aid this schooner, merchant ship, or whatever.

Peter Spectre: Which had priority, the picketing duty or the—?

Admiral O'Neill: No, the distress work. Because very often there would be a destroyer on duty out there on patrol with no boat to picket. He would be selected to go, because your other one would stay with the job of picketing his supply ship. But if they were all picketing a supply ship and a ship was in distress, one of them would go, because that took priority. It had to.

Peter Spectre: How did our territorial limits limit you in your activities?

Admiral O'Neill: Well, this type of rum patrol that I was on didn't limit us at all, because we were way offshore. The 12-mile limit you speak of?

Peter Spectre: Right.

Admiral O'Neill: No, it didn't bother us at all; we never worked in there.

Peter Spectre: No, I mean you were outside the 12-mile limit, so that—in other words, you couldn't seize one of these ships out there?

Admiral O'Neill: Oh, no. Oh, no. You couldn't seize them.

Peter Spectre: What I'm trying to ask, did you ever have any friction with the rumrunners up there, even though there was an international law against friction?

Admiral O'Neill: Well, we had no friction, but very often we would run up close to one of these ships, and some very uncomplimentary remarks would be passed back and forth between the crew and the people on the rumrunner. They would, as I say, say unkind things about each other. No, no. I think I know what you are leading up to there, but it didn't happen with us. Some of the ships out there, they would throw bolts and nuts at them and squirt the fire hose on them when they'd run up real close to them and things like that. Harassment, that's all it was. I heard about that, but it never happened on any ships I was on, because that was childish.

Peter Spectre: We heard about some of the ships out there would tow along a cable and try to foul it in the other ship's propeller. Did you ever hear—?

Admiral O'Neill: No, I never have, but I wouldn't doubt it. I wouldn't doubt it a bit.

Peter Spectre: What was your feeling about the law itself that you were protecting? You know and I know that a majority of the people during that time were openly against Prohibition.

Admiral O'Neill: That's right.

Peter Spectre: How did your and your fellow Coastguardsmen feel about not only the law but about the opposition in the country to the law, and the open aiding and abetting of the rumrunners and so forth?

Admiral O'Neill: Well, that's a good point. Of course, I'm speaking for myself, but I think the majority of the Coast Guard officers assigned to that duty realized that it was love's labor lost. We weren't stopping the inflow of whiskey, maybe slowing it down a little, as I said before, but we were given the job. We were carrying out a job that had been passed on to us, and all we could do was say, "Aye, aye, sir." and go ahead and carry it out to the best of our ability, and that's what we did.

But the Coast Guard came into some serious criticism by newspaper editors, writers, and all. We were supposed to be the people at fault, with all this trouble about Prohibition and all, because we were in the headlines, patrolling, stopping the rumrunners and all that. As one editorial writer once told me, "You know, we like the Coast Guard, but we print what we think the people like to read." Well, anyway, it wasn't good for the Coast Guard as far as the public was concerned. It was good experience for those of us assigned to it and those on shore, the staff and all. It was good staff duty; it was good experience for them, but in many ways it was a waste of money.

Peter Spectre: Before that time and after that time the Coast Guard was more or less out of the limelight. I think now it's becoming more in the limelight again, but before that time and immediately after that time, the Coast Guard was more or less the silent service. Did you have a difficult time adjusting to all this instant fame and notoriety and so forth?

Admiral O'Neill: No, I would say no difficulty adjusting. It was just something that had been due us for a long time—I mean, the good news about us. Prior to World War I days and between World War I and the rum war and all, we were, as you say, a silent service, practically unheard of. The things that were written about us in the papers and magazines were encouraging and proper and pleasing for us to read, you might say. It was only occasionally when we would rescue some ship or tow some disabled ship in that we got any good publicity. Then in this deluge of bad publicity during the rum days, then after that was over, we went back to being a silent service again until World War II exploded. Then after World War II I think we reaped some of the good publicity that was long overdue.

Peter Spectre: Will you tell me a little bit about during that time the Coast Guard more or less expanded from what it was before, because of the extra duties required by Customs work, and so more ships were added to the service, and consequently more men were needed to man these ships. Can you tell me about the source of the new officers that came into the Coast Guard and what your feelings were about new officers that were assigned?

Admiral O'Neill: Well, that expansion you refer to, that meant more enlisted men and more commissioned officers. More than we had available, more than the Academy could turn out in those days, so we commissioned a great many—I don't recall the exact number—men from civilian life and brought them in as commissioned officers. A great many were men who'd had experience in merchant ships and aboard yachts and things like that. They weren't just somebody from the Middle West who'd never seen a rowboat or a canoe. They were men who'd had some seagoing experience. They performed very, very well. There was a time when there was some feeling, that's natural, between the regular officers, the Academy officers, and these newly acquired officers where they were just commissioned overnight. After a while that feeling began to subside, and I think eventually it was forgotten entirely, because those officers that we brought in were high-caliber men. They were college men, and they performed very creditably in the service.

Peter Spectre: Did most of them stay in the service?

Admiral O'Neill: Most of them did, yes. Most of them stayed in the service, and some of them rose to flag rank. Oh, there were one or two, I think, that resigned for various reasons, but I don't recall any of the details.

Peter Spectre: Also, during this period there was a proposal to make the Coast Guard part of the Navy. I believe that Franklin Roosevelt had something to do with this.[*] Some people have said that the reason why was that the Coast Guard had so much extra money because of the needs of the rum duty. Do you remember anything about that period of time?

Admiral O'Neill: Well, on that subject I can go back to the time when I was a cadet. The old saying, you know, "When I was a cadet—" There was a movement underfoot then to keep the Coast Guard in the Navy. We were in the Navy then, because I was appointed a cadet by the Secretary of the Navy, Josephus Daniels.[†]

Peter Spectre: That was because of the First World War?

Admiral O'Neill: That's World War I I'm talking about now. And occasionally, and all through my career and up until I guess maybe the present day. I can't speak affirmatively about that.

Every so often, there would be some kind of movement underfoot to transfer the Coast Guard to the Navy. That has come up, I know, at least eight or ten times. I mean, spoken but not seriously. For various reasons. Some say, "You don't belong in the Treasury Department. You're more military than you are Customs collectors. You ought

---

[*] Franklin D. Roosevelt had served as Assistant Secretary of the Navy during the Wilson Administration, 1913-1921. He ran unsuccessfully for Vice President in 1920 and successfully for Governor of New York in 1928. He was elected President in 1932.

[†] Josephus Daniels served as Secretary of the Navy from 5 March 1913 to 5 March 1921, during both of President Woodrow Wilson's terms. The guided missile frigate *Josephus Daniels* (DLG-27), later redesignated a cruiser, was named for him.

to go over in the Navy where you belong." And congressmen make speeches about it. Magazines and newspapers would write about it—that's where we should go. And there was some argument put up about the money that we got, the expansion during the rum patrol.

And, of course, about 15-16 years ago, maybe more than that, there was a commission appointed that recommended various government reorganizations. One was that part of the Coast Guard should go back to Commerce, and part should go to the Navy, and break them up. Well, that fell apart. That was dropped during the Eisenhower Administration.[*] One of the problems there in 1953, when Eisenhower came in, the new Secretary of the Treasury wanted to know why we belonged in the Treasury Department.[†] We spent months trying to convince him that the Treasury Department was a logical place for the service, not because we had always been there; that wasn't so important. Finally that was dropped.

As I say, of course, I have no real knowledge about it now, but there is a question nowadays about whether the Department of Transportation is the proper place for it.[‡] No objections, as far as I've heard, were raised at taking the Coast Guard from the Treasury and putting it in Transportation. As far as money-wise is concerned, I don't know the exact budget figures, but I think probably the Coast Guard budget is many times over the other offices of Transportation. But that will come about in the future. Every so often it will come to life again.

Peter Spectre: I imagine it is very difficult, because the Coast Guard work cuts across many different missions and departments and so forth. There' law enforcement and military readiness and search and rescue and merchant marine safety. And each one of these things is more or less involved in other agencies' work, so I can see where it would be very difficult.

---

[*] Dwight D. Eisenhower served as President of the United States, 20 January 1953 to 20 January 1961.
[†] George M. Humphrey served as Secretary of the Treasury from 21 January 1953 to 29 July 1957.
[‡] When the cabinet-level Department of Transportation was created in January 1967, the Coast Guard was moved into the new department.

Admiral O'Neill: But it's much more effective and efficient if it's all in one organization and under one roof, as it is today. It's far, far better than if it's scattered all over the city of Washington, the way it used to be.

Peter Spectre: I heard that during the expansion, during the rum patrolling, when the subject was brought up of putting the Coast Guard into the Navy that the Coast Guard Academy Alumni Association came into the fray and because of that became a stronger alumni association, where before that time it had been more or less a loose, weak organization. Do you know anything about that?

Admiral O'Neill: I know very little, but I do know there's something to that. There is some substance to that story, but I don't know any of the details. I do know that there was a number of meetings held by sort of makeshift groups of Academy graduates in various parts of the country. They'd get together aboard ship, and it was like starting small lodges and clubs. It was kind of like the club idea. That was going on for a while during the rum patrol days.

Peter Spectre: Did you belong to—?

Admiral O'Neill: No, but I attended one of the meetings. It didn't amount to anything, one meeting on one of the large cutters. Nobody was invited but Academy graduates to this meeting. There were only about 15 or 20 there, but I never attended any other, because they were excluding some of these officers that we had taken in from the outside. I had three or four of them aboard my destroyer, and they were good officers. I didn't think much of the idea. I felt it was perfectly proper to make them members of the alumni association as honorary members or some kind of member like that. I was in favor of that, but not to exclude them. All of the regulars get together in a huddle, very secretly and all, and leave the others outside. I didn't go along with that at all. It died out, because it was a cockeyed idea to begin with. Foolish.

Peter Spectre: Admiral, could you tell me a little bit about how your experiences in the Navy destroyers given to the Coast Guard helped you develop in the Coast Guard?

Admiral O'Neill: Well, I think the experiences with a group of ships of that kind and the type of sea duty that we experienced, winter and summer, came in handy. I leaned on some of the knowledge and experience that I gained in those days later on aboard ship during World War II and associating with more officers and more men during the destroyer force days than I'd ever had occasion to do before. Some of the ships that I was on prior to the rum days, we had small crews, but the knowledge that I gained—you might say personnel management, handling the men, dealing with the officers during the rum days—came in handy later.

Peter Spectre: You said that you became a commanding officer of the *Ericsson* after being the executive officer. Did you expect to become commanding officer? What rank were you then?

Admiral O'Neill: I was a lieutenant, a two-striper.

Peter Spectre: Was it commonplace to be put in command as a lieutenant of a ship that size?

Admiral O'Neill: Well, at first I was assigned commanding officer while I was a lieutenant. Then I made lieutenant commander while I was on the *Ericsson*.

Peter Spectre: What about the other destroyers? What rank were the commanding officers?

Admiral O'Neill: They were lieutenant commanders and commanders.

Peter Spectre: So you were probably the most junior person on a destroyer in command.

Admiral O'Neill: Well, there at one time I think I probably was. I couldn't answer that definitely.

Peter Spectre: What did it feel like to be a lieutenant and command a destroyer? It would be the same thing, I suppose, as someone my age commanding a destroyer. I'd be a little nervous about it.

Admiral O'Neill: Well, it was, as they say, a challenge, but it was exciting, and I didn't have any qualms about it. Oh, I was nervous at times—of course, I was—because I wanted to do a good job; everybody does. I didn't want to run the ship aground or collide with another one or have any trouble like that. I was lucky. Duty like we had during the destroyer force days was bound to be extremely helpful to all the officers aboard for later on in their careers. I know even today, when I meet some of what I call us old-timers, our conversation will drift back to the destroyer force days. It was a new type of a ship for us to begin with, characteristics entirely different. The organization was similar but not exactly like the cutter days. Other than that, I don't know that can enlarge on that.

Peter Spectre: What happened to you when your period on the destroyers ended? You said that you were on more than one destroyer after the *Ericsson*, a couple of other ones. Were those also based in New London?

Admiral O'Neill: Yes, for a while, and then I was transferred to a destroyer that was based in Boston.

Peter Spectre: What was the name of that one?

Admiral O'Neill: That was the *Cassin*.[*]

---

[*] USS *Cassin* (later DD-43), name ship of her class of destroyers, was commissioned 9 August 1913. She had a standard displacement of 1,020 tons, was 305 feet long, and 30 feet in the beam. Her top speed was 30 knots. She was armed with four 4-inch guns, and eight 18-inch torpedo tubes. She was decommissioned by the Navy on 7 June 1922 and transferred to the Coast Guard on 28 April 1924. She was commissioned by the Coast Guard on 30 August 1924 with the new hull number of CG-1.

Peter Spectre: Did your wife move with you to Boston?

Admiral O'Neill: Yes, I was also transferred to a destroyer there in Boston, the *Monaghan*; she was to go out of commission. We took her down to Philadelphia to take over another destroyer, a newer type, what they called the flush deck. See, these destroyers I've been talking about were we called the broken deck. They had the high forecastle. We put the *Monaghan* out of commission and took over the *Herndon*. She was then being reconditioned for service as a rum patrol offshore cutter. When she was commissioned, we took her back to Boston, and I was only aboard for a short time. Then, when I transferred to the *Cassin*, I had command of her for about a year. Then I was transferred to the Coast Guard Academy as an instructor. My wife and children—we had two children by that time—moved back to New London.

Peter Spectre: Your wife probably enjoyed your service life so far, spending most of her time in New London.

Admiral O'Neill: Yes, well, her parents lived there, of course, and it was hometown for her and hometown for me, because I'd spent quite a bit of time there too. Two and a half years there as a cadet. It was hometown.

Peter Spectre: Was the Coast Guard Academy still at Fort Trumbull, or had it moved across the river?

Admiral O'Neill: No, no, it was still Fort Trumbull.

Peter Spectre: When did they move to their present site?

Admiral O'Neill: They moved to the present site, I think, in 1937.[*] Then the old Fort Trumbull, I think, was taken over by a branch of the University of Connecticut. Now I

---

[*] The Coast Guard Academy was moved to its current location in New London in 1932.

think it's a naval installation. I think the Navy's taken it over; I'm not certain about that.*

Peter Spectre: What year were you assigned to the Coast Guard Academy?

Admiral O'Neill: Nineteen twenty-eight.

Peter Spectre: So that Prohibition was still on, and the Coast Guard was still engaged in rum patrols?

Admiral O'Neill: Yes.

Peter Spectre: What were your duties at the Academy?

Admiral O'Neill: Well, I was an instructor and also commandant of cadets.

And then on one of the summer training cruises, the destroyer *Shaw* was assigned to the Academy as the training ship, along with the *Alexander Hamilton*, which was an old Navy ship of steam and sail. Those two ships made a cruise with cadets aboard, training, to several European ports. They were two radically different kinds of training ships. One was a destroyer, and one was an old steam and sail ship. The way we divided that up, we would assign a certain number of cadets to make the cruise, say, put half of them aboard the *Shaw*, the destroyer, and the other half aboard the *Hamilton*. Then, when they arrived in foreign ports such as London or Cherbourg, they would switch. They would transfer so they would have half their summer cruise, duty, and experience aboard the two different types of ships.

Peter Spectre: Did you go along as an instructor?

Admiral O'Neill: I wore two hats. I was the exec on the *Shaw* and also did some instructing. Most of the instructing was done by two or three of the officers who were

---

* From about 1950 to 1990 Fort Trumbull was the site of the Naval Underwater Sound Laboratory.

assigned specifically for the instruction work. But practically all stood watches and duties of that type.

Peter Spectre: What did you teach at the Academy and on the cruises?

Admiral O'Neill: I taught physics at the Academy and was also commandant of cadets. That was mostly paperwork and supervising the activities of the cadets, the procurement of clothing, and leave requests, and handling some of the punishments that some of the cadets sometimes earned. Also, I had what in those days we called tactics. It was mostly drill regulations, infantry drill paradings, and I guess some landing force exercises. Those were mostly my principal duties during—

Peter Spectre: Had the Academy grown since you had been there?

Admiral O'Neill: Oh, yes, yes. I was trying to think the other day how many were there when I went back as an instructor. I would say maybe 100 or 150; they had grown that much. Which is small compared to today. But on my last assignment there, I think that was a three-year assignment?

Peter Spectre: Did you enjoy it?

Admiral O'Neill: Oh, yes, I enjoyed it. I had to work hard. I had to study hard. I had to study harder than the cadets, because I had to keep ahead of them.

Peter Spectre: I've heard that a lot.

Admiral O'Neill: Well, it's so true. It's an oft-repeated remark, but it is true. I wasn't the only one that had to do that. You see, practically all the instructors then were regular officers, and we still had the same old civilian mathematics professor when I went back as when I was a cadet. I think he was still the only civilian there. The rest of us were regular officers.

Peter Spectre: Did you have any training when you first got there in teaching? Well, you spent two years in normal school, so you probably were pretty well qualified to—

Admiral O'Neill: Well, I had some of that, yes, but when I was transferred there I told the superintendent of the Academy, "Look, I'm really not qualified to teach these boys. I've had physics as a cadet at the Academy and in high school, but I haven't any special qualifications to teach a subject such as that. I can handle the rest of it all right.

"Well," he said, "you'll get along all right. You just burn the midnight oil and study hard, and you won't have any trouble teaching these lads." Well, I didn't exactly agree with him, but it worked out all right.

Peter Spectre: I guess nowadays a commissioned officer assigned as an instructor at the Academy usually has postgraduate training in some field.

Admiral O'Neill: That's right; that's right.

Peter Spectre: Did any of the instructors who taught with you during that period of time have any postgraduate training?

Admiral O'Neill: No, none to my knowledge.

Peter Spectre: Had anybody ever brought up the subject that it might be worthwhile?

Admiral O'Neill: Well, it was discussed occasionally, but nothing was ever done about it in those days. It was discussed amongst the instructors that it would be fine. In other words, my own case, for example, if I could have gone someplace and taken a year's course in the subject of physics, then I would have felt I was much better qualified to teach physics to the cadets and know where I was. As I say, I was just trying to keep ahead of them.

Peter Spectre: After seeing West Point, going to West Point for a period of time, and going to the Coast Guard Academy and teaching at the Coast Guard Academy, how do you think that they stacked up?

Admiral O'Neill: Well, of course, back in those days I think there was a much closer relationship at the Coast Guard Academy between the instructors and the cadets than at, say, West Point, where there was no friendly—you'd not call it cooperation, between the class and the instructors there. At West Point, the Military Academy, in mathematics, for example, the instructor would give each cadet a problem to solve on the blackboard. If the cadet wanted to change something, he couldn't erase anything on it without turning around and getting the permission of the instructor, who sat up at the end of the room. He might want to erase an X and substitute a Y; he couldn't do that unless he asked the instructor's permission.

Professor Dimick, the mathematics instructor at the Coast Guard Academy, would come in the room, sit down, and say to everybody, "Seats." Then he wanted to know if anyone had any questions to ask, if you'd had any trouble with any of the assignments he gave you yesterday. If a cadet would raise his hand and get up and say, "Well, this is what I didn't understand," the professor would go to the blackboard and show him what he did do right and how he should have solved the equation. Then he would ask someone else. He would help the cadets. In that way I think he was a teacher, whereas at the Military Academy, if you didn't know it when you went in there, well, you just didn't know it. The instructor wouldn't help you. He'd tell you to solve that equation. If you couldn't solve it, then you're out. I cite that as an example.

Another—like, well, for example, seamanship. I'm talking now about the cadets at the Coast Guard Academy. The seamanship instructor was always an experienced officer with many years' service. He might be a lieutenant, but he'd had many years' service. Promotion was slow in those days. He might be a lieutenant commander. And if a cadet didn't understand some part of seamanship, if he didn't understand what that meant, the instructor would explain it to him, go into the background of it. That's what I mean by a closer relationship between the instructor and the cadets.

Peter Spectre: What about discipline at the Coast Guard Academy? Was it stern?

Admiral O'Neill: Yes, we had good discipline, excellent discipline.

Peter Spectre: Were the instructors involved in that, or were the upper classes the disciplinarians?

Admiral O'Neill: Well, both, both. The upper classmen did some, and the instructors did some. We had a demerit system there at the Coast Guard Academy, but we had no serious disciplinary problems. There may have been one or two during the three years that I was there bounced out for disciplinary reasons, but it was very rare.

Peter Spectre: What about the attrition rate when you were an instructor? You said in your class you started with 15 and ended up with four. What about when you were an instructor, the classes that were there—was the attrition rate greater or lesser?

Admiral O'Neill: Less. It was greater during World War I, at the end of World War I. That's when, I say, maybe some of them were just there doing time. I think a few were there who had no intention whatsoever of following the Coast Guard as a career.

Peter Spectre: I've heard of all sorts of schemes for beating the draft, but that's the first time I've heard of that particular one?

Admiral O'Neill: I think it was true in many cases, though, as I say, there were some in my class I think wanted to make the service a career but couldn't make the grade, and there were some that were coasting.

Peter Spectre: What was life like at the Coast Guard Academy when you were an instructor?

Admiral O'Neill: The social life?

Peter Spectre: Yes, just general all around. Was it a good assignment?

Admiral O'Neill: It was an excellent assignment for the officers. New London was a Coast Guard town, as they used to call it, and there were ample social activities. Fort Trumbull wasn't what the Academy is today, but it was a picturesque place. It wasn't in what you might call the best section of New London, but we had our own little compound there. There were officers' quarters for about four or five families; the rest would have to live in town. Just the senior officers lived in the quarters there. For the cadets the social activities were, I thought, ample. They could go on liberty. They had plenty of liberty. They had dances. They all had to go to some church on Sunday. Now I understand there's some movement underfoot to eliminate that if the person so desires. But new London was a good liberty port, a good liberty port.

Peter Spectre: Well, your total service up until that time was sea service.

Admiral O'Neill: That was my first shore duty.

Peter Spectre: Did you look forward to that, or did you—I know some people when you take them off a ship, they just kind of get along in a shore assignment, whereas in other areas it's just the reverse.

Admiral O'Neill: Well, no, I think most of us adjusted very well to it. No, it was different, another new challenge. Of course, with young officers like that, it was always a thrill to get back aboard ship, and the lure of the sea had some effect. I think some of the older officers felt they'd had their tour at sea. That was sufficient for them, and they preferred the shore duty. But it was a good change.

Interview Number 2 with Admiral Merlin O'Neill, U.S. Coast Guard (Retired)
Place: Admiral O'Neill's home in Lusby, Maryland
Date: Saturday, 4 April 1970
Interviewer: Peter Spectre

Peter Spectre: Admiral, the last time we talked you were commanding destroyers in Boston. I wonder if you could pick up from there, explaining how you were transferred from Boston, and the last part of your tour of duty there.

Admiral O'Neill: My tour of duty of destroyers ended the summer of 1933, when I received orders to Baltimore, Maryland to command the CGC *Apache*.[*] I drove from Boston to Baltimore with my wife Esther and my two daughters, Patricia and Marilyn. We arrived in Baltimore on July the fourth, 1933, when the temperature was 104 degrees. My tour of duty on the *Apache* lasted about two and a half years.

Peter Spectre: Was this duty you requested?

Admiral O'Neill: No, this was not by request. The *Apache*'s duties, primarily, during the two and a half years, were regatta patrolling during the summer, assistance work, and we were particularly busy in the fall of 1933 when one of the severest hurricanes hit the East Coast. It came straight up Chesapeake Bay, and there was tremendous damage to small boats and buildings along the shoreline. We were kept busy all during that hurricane and for weeks afterward assisting boats that had been wrecked and searching for missing persons.

Also, a great deal of our time was taken during the hunting season searching for lost duck hunters. They would go out with their boats to a duck blind and not secure the boat properly. Then the tide would come up, the boat would drift away, and they would be marooned. We would get frantic calls from wives and relatives that certain people

---

[*] USCGC *Apache* had originally been commissioned as the *Galveston* on 22 August 1891. She was an iron-hulled, twin-screw ship, 190 feet long and 416 tons. Early in the 20th century was rebuilt and her name changed on 30 December 1904 to *Apache*. Her career from then on was mostly in the Chesapeake Bay area. Her Coast Guard service ended in 1937, and the U.S. Army later took her over.

were missing. We did a great deal of that and, as I say, regatta patrolling, and search and rescue and assistance work, and boarding—the usual Coast Guard activities.

Peter Spectre: What kind of ship was the *Apache*?

Admiral O'Neill: The *Apache* was a cutter about 185 feet long, an old ship, and she was built for interior waters like sounds and the bay. Most of her duties were in Chesapeake Bay.

Peter Spectre: Do you know when she was built?

Admiral O'Neill: I don't recall when she was built. About two years after I was transferred from her, she was surveyed, decommissioned, and sold to the Boston Iron and Metal Company in Baltimore, owned by a man by the name of Shapiro, I think. About that time the Army was looking for a boat to use down in the Pacific, so they bought this cutter from the Boston Iron and Metal Company and re-engined her. They took out the forward crew's quarters to make storage space for cargo, put in diesel engines, and took her down to the South Pacific. During World War II, when I was in the Pacific, I met someone who had seen the *Apache* down around the Solomon Islands and being used by the Army as a freight boat. What happened to her after that, I've never heard.[*]

Peter Spectre: How many men were on the *Apache*?

Admiral O'Neill: We had a crew of about 40. We had three commissioned officers and two warrant officers.

Peter Spectre: About the hurricane, I think that sounds pretty interesting to me. Can you tell me something about it, how it happened?

---

[*] In October 1944 the former cutter was used as a radio transmitter ship. She relayed the broadcast of General Douglas MacArthur's "I have returned" speech from the Philippines. She was scrapped in 1950.

Admiral O'Neill: Well, it was a typical West Indies hurricane. One thing that caused so much damage was the fact that the center of the storm came up the bay, and it caused a tremendous storm pattern. It's sometimes erroneously referred to as a tidal wave. It's the storm blowing and pushing the water up ahead of it. At the pier where we were moored, at Fort McHenry in Baltimore, the water came up four feet above the top of the pier, so it was about an eight-foot rise in the normal tide. Then, of course, with the hurricane winds of over 75 miles an hour, that is where much of the damage was caused, particularly along the western shore of Chesapeake Bay.

Peter Spectre: Were you at your dock when the hurricane came?

Admiral O'Neill: We were at the dock when it started and the tide began coming in so high. We realized we couldn't stay there, so we got under way. We went out into the mouth of the Patapsco River, where we anchored for a few hours. But we didn't stay there long, because we immediately began to get distress calls from our headquarters in Norfolk. They would receive the distress message by telephone from the Baltimore area, and they would relay that information back to us. Then we would know where to go and what to look for and what to search for and so forth. As I say, we were busy there, not only during the hurricane but for two or three weeks afterward.

Peter Spectre: Were there any other Coast Guard cutters in the Chesapeake?

Admiral O'Neill: We were the only one.

Peter Spectre: Not even in the lower Chesapeake?

Admiral O'Neill: Down in the lower bay near Norfolk. We were operating primarily in the upper part of the bay. You might say it was mostly north of the Potomac River—from there all the way to the north end of the bay.

Peter Spectre: Where did you live?

Admiral O'Neill: We lived in Stoneleigh, a residential section outside of Baltimore.

Peter Spectre: Was it a difficult change for you and your family to move from Boston down to Baltimore and set up a new home?

Admiral O'Neill: No, it was a pleasant move, and we enjoyed our tour of duty there. We had wonderful neighbors, and being in the service, as you well know, when you move into a strange locality, you have to make your own friends. In those days, there were no service people closer than Curtis Bay.* But we enjoyed our tour there very much, and I considered it one of the most interesting tours of duty I had while I was on sea duty.

Peter Spectre: What else happened while you were there, during those two and a half years?

Admiral O'Neill: Nothing that I can recall of extraordinary. It was primarily routine. One thing that was somewhat different was the frequency of the calls that we would get, particularly during the hunting season and during the icebreaking season. We were called on to do quite a bit of icebreaking. The ship didn't have the weight and the horsepower to be as effective as modern icebreakers are today of that size. We have harbor tugs now, smaller than the *Apache*, that are more efficient as icebreakers, because they have more horsepower and heavier plating. I recall one month of February, I think it was February of '34, we had 28 calls for assistance. Sometimes we were under way already when we would get these calls. The only time we went back into port was to take on coal—she was a coal burner—and fresh water, some provisions, and then go right back out.

Peter Spectre: What type of craft did your assistance cases involve? Were they mostly fishing boats?

---

* The Coast Guard Yard is at Curtis Bay, Maryland, near Baltimore.

Admiral O'Neill: Well, all sizes from yachts and rowboats and fishing boats and barges. One was a banana boat hauling bananas from Central America into Baltimore. I don't recall the company now—"Great White Fleet," did they call it?* She ran aground over on the eastern shore, somewhere near Sharp's Island, and we were sent over by district headquarters in Norfolk to see if we could get her off the sandbar.

When we arrived over there, she not only had a cargo full of bananas, but the deck was heaped with bananas. We tried to pull her off and were unsuccessful, so the captain radioed to his agent in Baltimore and requested permission to throw overboard the deck cargo of bananas. He was granted that permission, so for the next several hours the crew of the ship, probably a freighter, was busy throwing these huge stalks of bananas over into the bay. The bay was covered with floating bananas. Of course, our crew had a Roman holiday, because they would fish them out of the water and pile them on the *Apache* so they could take them home with them. We finally got the ship off after they had lightened her by discharging the deck cargo. She went on her way to Baltimore, and we followed along behind her with our cargo of bananas that they had jettisoned and we had fished out of the water.

Peter Spectre: They didn't ask for them back?

Admiral O'Neill: No, so our crew each had a big stalk of bananas to take home with them.

Peter Spectre: You mentioned icebreaking. It comes as a surprise to hear that there is ice sometimes in the Chesapeake Bay in the wintertime. Was there more ice in the mid-'30s than there is now?

Admiral O'Neill: No. It was very heavy there for the winter of '34 and '35. We had to make the best efforts we could to break out these ships coming through the C&D Canal and going down the bay.† We worked up off the northern end of the bay, around Turkey

---

* Probably the United Fruit Company.
† C&D – Chesapeake and Delaware.

Point and in that area up there, trying to break a channel open so they could follow along behind us and get through. Sometimes we would get into trouble ourselves in getting out.

Peter Spectre: Are you familiar with the politics of icebreaking? At one time the Coast Guard didn't have an icebreaking mission, and then it was assigned to the Coast Guard by congressional act, I believe. Do you know if during that time icebreaking was a mission of the Coast Guard?

Admiral O'Neill: I don't recall that, but that was probably done before I was assigned to any type of ship that could break ice. It would come under the category of assisting maritime commerce. A ship getting caught in the ice is sometimes in danger, and it's an economic loss to everybody. It probably stemmed from assisting in that way.

Peter Spectre: There was a time when the Coast Guard didn't have an icebreaking mission. Then icebreaking first began as a request to assist commerce, and then it was officially made a mission of the service. But there was a period when ice was being broke even though it really wasn't a duty.

Admiral O'Neill: I'm well aware that it wasn't a duty many years ago, but I know nothing about the history of when or how it came about.

Peter Spectre: Was there anything else that's significant that happened to you?

Admiral O'Neill: At the moment I don't recall anything else of any particular importance.

Peter Spectre: You were a lieutenant commander then?

Admiral O'Neill: Yes.

Peter Spectre: In light of your later career, how do you think that this tour on the *Apache* helped you?

Admiral O'Neill: Well, it was a different type of experience. I'd never had that type of duty before. My duties before that have been mentioned, where I was a junior officer and on regular Coast Guard patrols and assistance work, but where I had an opportunity to gain experience in icebreaking and assistance work, and working during that famous hurricane of 1933. That was all good background experience.

Peter Spectre: I wasn't around then, but that storm destroyed a chimney on my father's house up in Massachusetts.

During this period of time and later on, there must have been people who helped you in furthering your career and eventually becoming Commandant of the Coast Guard. Were there any people you met, that you dealt with, or that you were assigned to duty with, who helped you later on, who proved to be an asset to help you move ahead in the service? Some people call them lucky breaks, and other people call them intentional happenings, but the people that you met, that you worked with, that helped you to move on in the service.

Admiral O'Neill: Of course, that's difficult to answer. I handled all the ranks from ensign up to admiral. I was fortunate in many ways in being aboard ship with senior officers whom I got along very well with and frankly liked me and undoubtedly gave me good fitness reports. There's one officer in particular I served with when I was an ensign aboard the *Gresham* in New York. That was my first assignment after I was commissioned in 1921. He was Admiral J. F. Farley.[*] He was the navigator aboard the *Gresham*. He was my predecessor, and he recommended me for appointment as Assistant Commandant in 1946. Then, when he retired in on December 31, 1949, prior to that he had recommended me as Commandant to succeed him. I had served with him many years before.

---

[*] In 1921 he was Lieutenant (junior grade) Joseph Francis Farley, USCG.

Peter Spectre: Did you serve with him at any period of time after that?

Admiral O'Neill: No, not after that, except for one short trip when the *Mojave* came around from Seattle to Philadelphia. He was the executive officer then, and I was the navigator, but that was just for the short trip around. Other than that, I've been with him on other assignments but not aboard ship or directly working for him. I've known him all those years.

Peter Spectre: When you were on the *Gresham* with him, he was a lieutenant?

Admiral O'Neill: I think he was a lieutenant, and I was fresh out of the Academy as an ensign.

Peter Spectre: Did you get to know him well? Was he a personal friend?

Admiral O'Neill: As well as a junior officer would know a senior officer. He was well senior to me. I don't recall what his rank was on the *Mojave* when we came around. I imagine he was a commander at that time.

Peter Spectre: What other people did you have contact with that you think maybe helped you in later years.

Admiral O'Neill: Well, it's hard to say. Some may have helped me that I never knew anything about.

Peter Spectre: How about before you went to Coast Guard Headquarters? Did you have any contact with Admiral Waesche?[*] He probably wasn't an admiral when you had contact with him.

---

[*] Admiral Russell R. Waesche, USCG, served as Commandant of the Coast Guard from June 1936 to December 1945. Initially in that post he was a rear admiral, promoted to vice admiral in March 1942 and four-star admiral in April 1945.

Admiral O'Neill: Yes, I knew him very well. I knew him on the West Coast when he was in command of a seagoing tug. Then I knew him when I was transferred from Baltimore to headquarters in 1935. I saw him off and on all the time he was in the service. Then, there at headquarters, I saw him frequently. When I was first transferred there in the office of operations, I was the assistant operations officer, and I had occasion to see him many times then. When he retired, Admiral Farley took over.[*]

Peter Spectre: The reason why I'm asking this type of question is because there are very few people who make Commandant in the Coast Guard. There's only one every four years, so I'm trying to get some idea how one goes about it. I'm sure you never set your mind and said, "I'm going to be Commandant and set a plan of how I'm going to carry it out." I'm sure it doesn't happen that way. But there must be certain key points that you can look back on and say, "This is something that helped me move in that direction," even though it might not have been intentional on your part, or even on someone else's part. You might have been in the right place at the right time, or gotten the right assignment, or something else along that line.

Admiral O'Neill: Well, I think it was undoubtedly very helpful to me being assigned to headquarters from 1935 to 1942.

Also, it was helpful to me in progress through the ranks to be assigned to Baltimore when I came back to shore duty from sea duty toward the end of the war. I was assigned over there as the section commander, where I had contacts with shipping people. The Coast Guard Yard was not under my command, but we had the training station, and the captain of the port was under my command and the beach patrol. Most of my contacts there were with the shipping people, and we all got along well. Apparently they liked me, and whether they ever put in a word for me or not, I don't know. I never will know. They may have spoken to some of the senior officers in headquarters about it; that's a possibility. It at least gave me the opportunity to become fairly well known in shipping circles, not only in Baltimore but New York as well, because some of the main

---

[*] Admiral Joseph F. Farley, USCG, served as Commandant of the Coast Guard from 1 January 1946 to 31 December 1949.

offices of the people there in Baltimore were in New York. So that tied in with the New York shipping circles.

Peter Spectre: Why don't we go on to your assignment after the *Apache*? Tell me a little bit about how it came about.

Admiral O'Neill: While I was on duty in Baltimore, there was a reorganization of the various offices and divisions of headquarters, and one of the new offices set up was the office of operations. One of the civilians hired to help in the reorganization of headquarters came over to Baltimore and came down to the *Apache* and told me about this and said that I was being considered for transfer to headquarters in the office of operations for offshore activities. There were two branches—the offshore and the inshore. I asked him why he seemed to think I was fitted for that particular duty, and he said, "You've had much experience in offshore Coast Guard operations, the various cutters that you've served on and the destroyer duty that you had here in the Atlantic."

So I said that was quite all right with me. So I passed the word on to Esther and my daughters that we might be moving to Washington in the very near future. We moved there in October 1935. Of course, that type of duty was strictly office work. It was my job to get out orders, for example, setting up the Bering Sea patrol, writing the orders and asking personnel to assign Bering Sea patrol commanders. Then writing orders to him and the orders to the ships to be assigned to duty in southeast Alaska and also the Bering Sea. It was strictly office work.

Peter Spectre: Before we get too deeply into it, can you tell me how headquarters was organized before you came?

Admiral O'Neill: I don't know very much about it. They had an operations officer who was a civilian employee. His name was Maxam.* He handled everything—the inshore patrol, the offshore patrol, sort of a one-man office, but the Coast Guard was growing a little bit and expanding, and I think improving, and they decided that we should

---

* Oliver M. Maxam, Chief of the Division of Operations, Coast Guard Headquarters.

modernize the entire structure, which they did. But I'm not familiar with what they had there before.

Peter Spectre: Did they change the whole organization of headquarters?

Admiral O'Neill: Most of it. The setting up of a new finance and supply office and inspection. It was pretty well reorganized.

Peter Spectre: How big was headquarters when you first were there?

Admiral O'Neill: I would estimate there were four 40 or 50 commissioned officers. The civilian personnel, I have no idea.

Peter Spectre: Do you have any idea, were there more civilians or less?

Admiral O'Neill: I think there were more civilian employees.

Peter Spectre: Where was Coast Guard Headquarters at that time?

Admiral O'Neill: That was at 15th and H Street. Then, shortly after that, we moved over to the Liberty Loan Building, 14th and Maine Avenue.

Peter Spectre: Where did you move your family to? Did you move from Baltimore to Washington?

Admiral O'Neill: Yes, we found a small house out in Bethesda, and we lived there for the next several years until the next tour of duty came along.

Peter Spectre: Can you explain to me some of the other things that you were involved in at headquarters? You became the chief director of the Auxiliary as your next assignment in headquarters. What happened up until then?

Admiral O'Neill: I was in operations until Admiral Waesche called me in one day and told me about this new organization that the Coast Guard was setting up, which was then known as that Coast Guard Reserve, and told me that he wanted me to head it up. He told me to get started on the organization of it and the rules and regulations and so forth.

Admiral Waesche received a letter about 1935 or '36 from a man on the West Coast whose name I do not recall. The name Malcolm rings a bell with me. Whether that was his first name or his last name, I don't recall. But he suggested that the Coast Guard establish a reserve consisting of yacht and small-boat owners to assist the Coast Guard in any type of work that they might be able to help the Coast Guard with, and also to promote safety in small boating.

That eventually led to drawing up a bill which was put through Congress and became law in 1937, creating this nonmilitary Coast Guard Reserve. Then there was a great deal of so-called spadework to be done. The potential members of this Coast Guard Reserve were a little bit leery of the organization, because when I would speak to a group such as a yacht club, to tell them that we were organizing this reserve and that it was nonmilitary, a great many of them were very skeptical. They were bound to be skeptical, because the war clouds were gathering over Europe about that time. I think the war had started in Poland, and they said, "The war clouds are gathering, and you say it's nonmilitary, but how do we know? You might change that, and we'd all be called into service that we don't look forward to."[*]

Then, when the war did come about, and we became more and more involved, and it was a certainty that we would soon be in it, the idea was to set up a military Coast Guard Reserve and change the name of the first Coast Guard Reserve, which was nonmilitary, to the Coast Guard Auxiliary. That was done through congressional action. Then, after deciding to have a military reserve, the question then was what name should we give to this nonmilitary organization of yachtsmen and small-boat owners that was designed primarily to make sure that the boats were operated safely and have more equipment than the law actually requires.

---

[*] World War II began on 1 September 1939, when German ground forces invaded Poland. Two days later Great Britain and France declared war on Germany. The civilian Coast Guard Reserve started in 1939.

So I contacted some of my friends in the Power Squadron, one of whom was Commodore Charles F. Chapman, who was one of the great small-boat owners and yachtsmen and commodores in the United States. He was the editor of the bible, as it's sometimes referred to, *Piloting, Seamanship, and Small Boat Handling*. I contacted him. I contacted a Navy admiral who was heading up the Navy Reserve in the Navy Department, and asked him if he had any suggestions about it. I told him what our problem was, and in talking to him and various people we got all kinds of suggestions about names, and finally came to the word "Auxiliary."

That was objected to at first, because it sounded like the ladies' society. They didn't want to be a member of any ladies' auxiliary in the Coast Guard. Well, that didn't amount to too much, and the name Auxiliary prevailed. It's that today and always will be, and it's a wonderful organization.

I had the good fortune of being the first chief commander. We started out, and I think the first flotilla was organized in Baltimore and the next one, I think, was organized in New York, then one in Norfolk, one in Washington. That's the way it started. Then it spread to the Midwest and the Pacific Coast. They came along rapidly after the first two or three flotillas were formed.

Peter Spectre: How did the people in the service react to this new thing, especially in the beginning when it was being discussed whether the Coast Guard Reserve would be the auxiliary, whether it should be formed, and what it should constitute, and so forth? I can imagine there was probably some pretty heated discussions.

Admiral O'Neill: Yes, there were heated discussions. There were a number of senior officers who were opposed to it, and some had no particular thought one way or the other. They weren't particularly enthusiastic about it. The most enthusiastic officer in the Coast Guard at the time was Admiral Waesche himself. He was all for it, and that indicates the wisdom that the man had at the time—the foresight. I sat in on conferences in Admiral Waesche's office, but I didn't have much to say. I was listening. They spoke outright in telling that they thought it was a mistake, and it would be a nuisance, and words like that. After it got started, then the trend changed, and more and more officers became interested in it, because they realized the high caliber of men that were coming in: businessmen, well-educated men, men high up in their organizations, and eventually it developed into one of our greatest assets.

Peter Spectre: Were you involved in the planning for it before you were assigned the specific duty of directing it?

Admiral O'Neill: Only in getting some of my friends to help in drafting the regulations for it. I had nothing to do with drawing up the bill that was sent to the Hill or any of the hearings.* Admiral Waesche carried the ball on all that. I don't know who helped him draw up the bill, but I know he actually did the speaking before the members of the congressional committees in the House and the Senate to explain to them what this was all about.

Peter Spectre: Was there any congressional controversy?

Admiral O'Neill: No. I didn't attend the hearings, but I understand that some had a great many questions to ask, naturally, because they were curious and wanted to know how much it would cost and things like that. The cost was so negligible that that was not a very serious point.

Peter Spectre: I'm curious about what the Coast Guard expected to gain from this.

Admiral O'Neill: Well, naturally, being always interested in the safety of the small-boat operating fields, to get small-boat operators and yachtsmen, whether they were members of the Auxiliary or not, to operate their boats more safely, and that was right down the line of the Coast Guard duties in those days. It would cut down on a lot of the work that we had to do. It wasn't a question of taking money out of our pockets. It was a question of getting a helping hand to carry out one of our duties, and that was it.

---

* "The Hill" refers to Capitol Hill in Washington, D.C., that is, the U.S. Congress.

Peter Spectre: One of the organizations that was directly affected by the formation of the Coast Guard Auxiliary was the U.S. Power Squadron. Right now the two organizations are competing for members. What were the Power Squadron's feelings about it? You must have had contact during that time.

Admiral O'Neill: Many of the Power Squadron members in those days were a little bit upset, because they said we were copying their organization. We were setting up an organization that would compete with them and compete unfairly, because ours was a federal organization, and theirs was strictly private. On the other hand, a great many accepted it in good faith and good feeling. I only know of one problem man in the Power Squadron; I haven't seen him since. He was quite vehement about it and made sarcastic comments about the Coast Guard Auxiliary at meetings of the Power Squadron, which I heard about later. I wasn't present. But I think, all in all, it was highly accepted, and I don't think there's been any difficulty about it since.

I know they have teaching courses, educational courses, and so do we, but our Auxiliary can help us patrol regattas and do small assistance work. This doesn't interfere with the Power Squadron. For instance, in Florida one lighthouse station down there had no boats. When a boat gets in trouble there near the light station, they call on the Auxiliary to come out and tow him in. It's been a tremendous help to us, and I think the principal thing is aiding in this boating safety. These so-called free inspections that they make of the boats—if they pass, they give them a decal. That means something to the yachtsmen, because when our boarding officers go out boarding, if they see the decal in the pilothouse window, they sometimes will say, "We don't need to go aboard there, because he's already been inspected by a competent Auxiliary man." They can go aboard and inspect the boat, but many times they'll check and see when it was pasted. If it's current, they tell him to go on his way.

Peter Spectre: Was there any consideration given to subsidizing the Power Squadron instead of involving yourself in organizing a brand-new group, the Coast Guard Auxiliary, merely taking over the Power Squadron and making it a part of the Coast Guard?

Admiral O'Neill: Not to my knowledge. If that was ever discussed, I never knew about it. It could have been, but I wouldn't have been in a position to know anything about it.

Peter Spectre: What about the timing of the formation of the group? You mentioned that some of the people were skeptical because of the possibility of this country being engaged in a war. Did the fact that the Coast Guard saw the possibility of being involved in a large-scale war determine whether a Coast Guard Auxiliary would be formed? Was that one of the reasons why it was formed?

Admiral O'Neill: No, I don't think so.

Peter Spectre: It was strictly for—

Admiral O'Neill: Because the first suggestion came in around 1935. That was long before—everybody was at peace in those days. A man from California wrote this letter to Admiral Waesche—I saw the letter—suggesting this reserve which became the Auxiliary, but there was no thought then of the United States being involved in war. In 1937 the clouds began to thicken a little bit, but they didn't get bad until '39, as I recall. That's when the Coast Guard Reserve began to militarize.

Peter Spectre: While you were in the office of operations at headquarters, before you became involved in the Coast Guard Auxiliary, were you making plans for the possibility of a war to come? Did you see the writing on the wall? Did you have any idea of what was going to happen, and did you make any plans for it?

Admiral O'Neill: No, not while I was in operations. Our activities there were primarily flood relief in the Mississippi and the high river areas. Every spring there was a flood there. That was one of the biggest jobs in operations and also the offshore normal activities of the cutters and the lifeboat stations along the coast. That was what I meant by the inshore patrol. We had no plans then of getting into a war or trying to get ourselves ready if we got into a war. Of course, the fact that later on, when we did get into it, some of our experiences on the destroyers came in handy, but there were no war plans to my knowledge in Coast Guard Headquarters back in '35 or '36, '37.

Peter Spectre: Was that detrimental to your future activities? Looking back, the war began, the Coast Guard came under the operational control of the Navy at the beginning of the war. Was your lack of preparation, organized, thoughtful preparation, detrimental? Did it hinder you in any way?

Admiral O'Neill: Well, you might say it was somewhat of a handicap, but we had never—not since World War I had we been closely connected with the Navy. Not like we'd be today, since World War II. I think that many of our ships that were taken over by the Navy and became a part of the Navy, had guns installed, heavier guns and more guns, and depth charges and all of these gadgets that had to go on. Nothing like that was done in preparation for it, so we weren't particularly well prepared for operation with the Navy as a seagoing, fighting ship, and I think that applies to lots of others too. I don't think the Navy was fully prepared themselves in all respects. You're never fully prepared. It's like when a captain of a ship receives his orders: "When in all respects ready, proceed to sea." He's never, in all respects, ready. So he proceeds to sea anyway. I think the fact that some of the Navy procedure was strange to us, bound to be, Navy regulations that ours were subject to, but I think our officers learned quickly and fitted in very well with the Navy operation.

Peter Spectre: When did the Coast Guard transfer to the Navy?

Admiral O'Neill: I guess that was just about Pearl Harbor Day. I'm not sure of the date.[*]

Peter Spectre: Were you involved in it in any way? You were no longer in operations?

---

[*] As authorized by Congress, on 1 November 1941 President Franklin D. Roosevelt ordered the Coast Guard to "operate as part of the Navy, subject to the orders of the Secretary of the Navy." The Coast Guard returned to the Treasury Department on 1 January 1946.

Admiral O'Neill: No, I was in the Coast Guard Auxiliary. I was the chief director. I guess it must have been right after—you see, to transfer over, all the President has to do is write his name on a piece of paper, and over we go.

Peter Spectre: Let's go back to the formation of the Coast Guard Auxiliary. I'd like to have you explain how you began. You were the first man, probably the only man for a while involved in it, at least Coast Guard officer involved. How did you begin? It must have been an unbelievable undertaking.

Admiral O'Neill: The first thing, of course, was to get the regulations written and then the assignment of officers as directors in each district. After a while we finally got officers in all the districts. They were supplied with copies of the regulations and all the information that we could possibly give them at the time as to what we expected of them. Then they, in turn, would meet with yacht club groups and small-boat organizations and tell them about this, about the Coast Guard Auxiliary, what it was, what it was for, and what we wanted to start a flotilla. Sometimes on individual would say he would be the flotilla commander, so he would directly appoint him the flotilla commander. Then, with the two of them working together, they would get others in and sign on the dotted line, so to speak. In that way it began to grow. We had flags manufactured and insignias prepared. It took many months to get the thing rolling, but once it started it began to grow and spread. It took a great deal of explaining. The directors helped the flotilla commander and the commodores and people that he would appoint, and people elected by their own people as officers, sell the idea to their own members. As soon as they found out that they weren't going to be drafted, it was clear sailing after that.

Peter Spectre: Did you have a staff to help you in this?

Admiral O'Neill: I had one yeoman. I called on other friends of mine to help me at times. I would also call in some of the district directors nearby, like Norfolk and New York, and have them come down to headquarters to help me. They were in close touch with the problems in the field, and they came up with excellent ideas that I'd never have thought of, because I was sitting at a desk in headquarters, and they were out in the field actually putting this thing across. I would say it worked out all right. It was a small organization. The paperwork was not voluminous. It wouldn't be like is today, of course. But as it grew and built up, then more personnel had to be added to the staff there at headquarters. Two people couldn't run it today, but they could to start with. They had to start small or slowly and gain speed and size after you get under way.

Peter Spectre: I've had many talks with Captain Tony Caliendo about the formation of the Auxiliary and so forth, and he played a key part, according to him.[*]

Admiral O'Neill: He did, especially in Chicago.

Peter Spectre: Could you tell me something about this?

Admiral O'Neill: I don't know the details on it, but the director that we sent out there—I don't know how he became acquainted with Captain Caliendo, but I do know that Captain Caliendo was a tremendous help to him in forming the first flotillas in Chicago. I know I attended a meeting there right in the very beginning, and that's the first time I met Captain Caliendo. That was before he came into the Coast Guard. He came in, I think, later on in the enlisted ranks in the military reserve and was fleeted up to where he is today—a captain.[†]

I attended this meeting in Chicago called by the district director, and Caliendo spoke at that meeting. He was very enthusiastic about it, and the director told me that Caliendo had been most helpful to him in contacting yachtsmen and what I called potential members. Then Caliendo eventually came to headquarters, and he served on one of the cutters. I think he came in as a chief boatswain's mate, and he was commissioned later on. I wasn't there when that took place.

---

[*] Captain Anthony J. Caliendo, USCG (Ret.)
[†] Caliendo was commissioned as a Coast Guard officer in 1949.

Peter Spectre: There were other things involved later on. The old Coast Guard Reserve became the Coast Guard Auxiliary at the beginning of the war. Then the temporary reserve became involved somewhere along the line. There's quite a bit of confusion about the three organizations, what the functions of each one were.

Admiral O'Neill: The Temporary Reserve came along after my time. The idea was to have this so-called Temporary Reserve that would come and wear the Coast Guard uniforms and handle primarily the patrol, like port security and some of the beach patrol activities. In Baltimore there was a Temporary Reserve organization there that stood guard at piers and warehouses and work of that kind. They wore regular Coast Guard uniforms. I have very little information about when it was formed and the details of it. I do know that there was a Temporary Reserve.

Peter Spectre: How many members of the Coast Guard were there at the beginning of the war?

Admiral O'Neill: I would say less than 500.

Peter Spectre: What about the Coast Guard Reserve, the military reserve? Did that start off small?

Admiral O'Neill: Yes. You see, when it first started we had no reserve training station at all. We had the commissioned men who had some sea experience, and we'd just call them in the office after they had been investigated and checked by intelligence. If their background was good, and they had to pass a physical exam, if they'd had some kind of experience, say, in the merchant marine, or yachtsmen at all, we'd put a uniform on them.

Then, later on, we took over a hotel in Florida and set up OCS school in New London, Connecticut, at the Coast Guard Academy. That was after my time too. I know there were at least one, and maybe two, hotels in Florida that were taken over for this indoctrination. I think they were given about a three months' course down there—I'm not sure about that—on how to wear the uniform and military etiquette, and courtesy, and simple things about service life and routine. So when they were transferred to a ship, they were pretty well prepared to step in and learn about shipboard duties and shore station activities while they were helping out aboard. And many of them turned out to be very excellent men.

Peter Spectre: During that time the Coast Guard was recruiting to expand because of the war. What made the difference between whether you were going to become a member of the regular Coast Guard or the Coast Guard Reserve, because it was active duty, any way you sliced it?

Admiral O'Neill: That's a question I'm not sure I can answer. I know we had plenty of applicants for enlistment, because a great many thought they were going to guard the coast. They didn't know they were going to wind up out in the South Pacific and the Mediterranean and all over the world. How that came about, I can't answer. Whether they said they wanted to enlist as regular Coast Guard, permanent establishment, or in the Reserve. That was a field that I had nothing to do with, and I'd hate to attempt to answer that question, because I might be entirely off base.

Peter Spectre: Do you know why you were selected to organize the Coast Guard Auxiliary?

Admiral O'Neill: No, I don't. Admiral Waesche just called me in his office one day and told me about what his plans were on this, and when he got the bill through, he wanted me to head it up and for me, in the meantime, to think about it and what kind of an organization it was going to require, and that's all—unless he said, "Eeeny, meeny, meiny, mo."

Peter Spectre: What were your personal feelings about it?

Admiral O'Neill: Well, I thought it was a change; it was something new. You know the famous saying, a challenge? I always accepted different types of duty in an optimistic frame of mind. I'd know nothing about them, but I thought, "Well, learn while you were growing."

Peter Spectre: You were there at headquarters for quite a while and spent a good portion of the time behind a desk. Were you ready to move out? Were you excited about going to sea, for instance? Did you want to leave?

Admiral O'Neill: Oh, yes. You see, I was there in operations and as chief director of the Auxiliary and as heading up the Reserve at the beginning, that is, for the commissioning of officers. I was there altogether, on these three assignments, almost seven years. Maybe that's one reason Admiral Waesche picked me, because I was handy.

Peter Spectre: You were also the first head of the military Coast Guard Reserve?

Admiral O'Neill: Yes, right in the beginning, when we were taking in these people that I mentioned. We had no training station set up for them. But, of course, after Pearl Harbor those of us in headquarters knew that we were going to be ordered to sea eventually, and we thought, "Well, why not? That's our profession; we're supposed to go to sea." So I was all ready for it, but I got very short orders. That was the only thing that upset me. The personnel officer called me into his office and said, "I want you to leave tomorrow morning and go down to Norfolk and relieve [a certain officer on a certain ship]." And that was at noontime. That was the only thing that I was very bitter about, not to go to sea. If I'd been given 24 hours more or two days' warning so I could have gotten my clothing together and straightened up some of my personal affairs, and not dumped everything into Esther's lap and say, "Here it is; I've got to move." That was it, but it turned out all right. I got over it, but I was very much upset about it at the time.

Peter Spectre: What was the assignment?

Admiral O'Neill: That was a Navy transport, the *Leonard Wood*.[*]

Peter Spectre: This wasn't a Coast Guard ship at all?

Admiral O'Neill: No, it was an Army transport taken over by the Navy and run by the Coast Guard.

Peter Spectre: Who was on it before you arrived? Was it a Navy officer?

Admiral O'Neill: No, a Coast Guard officer.

Peter Spectre: So it had already been in operation by the Coast Guard?

Admiral O'Neill: Oh, yes. There was a Coast Guard officer on it originally when they took her over just as a straight transport, just hauling troops. Then he was transferred to some other sea duty, and the ship was laid up for a while to convert her into a combat loader for the amphibious work.[†] Most of the ship's time in the war was in the amphibious force, not straight transports, what was sometimes referred to as the seagoing ferryboats, that is, hauling troops from New York to Liverpool, or New York to Plymouth, or whatever it may be. I was transferred there in 1942.

Peter Spectre: Did you ever hear the name of the officer that was there before you?

Admiral O'Neill: Zoole.[‡]

---

[*] USS *Leonard Wood* (AP-25), a former merchant ship, became an Army transport, and then was acquired by the Navy on 3 June 1941. She was commissioned 10 June 1942 with a Coast Guard crew. Her first commanding officer as a Navy ship was Commander Harold G. Bradbury, USCG, who had been a year ahead of O'Neill at the Coast Guard Academy. The 21,900-ton transport was 535 feet long, 72 feet in the beam, had a maximum draft of 31 feet, and a maximum speed of 17.5 knots. The Coast Guard operated the ship until 1946, when she returned to the Army.
[†] USS *Leonard Wood* entered the Philadelphia Navy Yard in March 1942 to be converted to an attack transport. She was redesignated APA-12 on 1 February 1942.
[‡] Captain Ephraim Zoole, USCG, Coast Guard Academy class of 1920.

Peter Spectre: What was your rank then?

Admiral O'Neill: I was a commander.

Peter Spectre: Can you tell me something about what it was like? How big was the ship?

Admiral O'Neill: She was one of the old Munson Liners.* She was 535 feet long, and the tonnage was something like 14,000 tons. To convert her from just a troop carrier they had to put on these landing boats, these LCVPs, and davits to handle them and hoisting gear.† And all the wood and furnishings had to be taken off that were flammable.

Peter Spectre: It was a luxury liner then?

Admiral O'Neill: She was a luxury liner, yes. I was transferred to her around the first of October in '42. When I joined the ship in Norfolk, they were loading troops to go up to Cove Point in the Chesapeake Bay for rehearsal, getting ready for the North African landing. Then we sailed shortly after that on this big convoy. I think those landings were in the month of November in '42 in North Africa.‡

Peter Spectre: The *Leonard Wood* was quite a bit different from any other ship that you had commanded.

Admiral O'Neill: Yes, she was larger.

Peter Spectre: Did you have a hard time adjusting to it?

---

* The ship was completed in 1922 as the *Nutmeg State* for the U.S. Shipping Board. That same year she was renamed *Western World* and managed by Munson Line. In 1926 she was sold to the Munson Line, and in 1938 the U.S. Maritime Commission took over Munson Line's fleet. In 1939 she went to the U.S. Army and became the *Leonard Wood*.

† LCVP – landing craft, vehicle and personnel.

‡ Allied forces invaded Casablanca in French Morocco on 8 November 1942. The *Leonard Wood* was one of four transports in near Cape Fedhala to send her boats to the beach at the beginning of the landings. For details see pages 58-65 of Samuel Eliot Morison, *Operations in North African Waters: October 1942-June 1943* (Boston: Little, Brown, 1947). It is Volume II of *History of United States Naval Operations in World War II*.

Admiral O'Neill: No, it wasn't too difficult. My first glimpse of the ship sort of flattened me a little bit, so to speak. I walked down the pier there at Norfolk about 7:00 or 8:00 in the morning, and the size of the ship was a little bit staggering. But after you get aboard and learn your way around, you become accustomed to it. I was fortunate in having many excellent officers, and several of them had been on there since the time she was first taken over as a regular troop carrier. We had a good crew.

Peter Spectre: How many men did you have in the crew?

Admiral O'Neill: Six hundred, plus 50 officers. It was a big organization.

Peter Spectre: What was everybody doing? For instance, with 50 officers were they all standing watch?

Admiral O'Neill: Well, there were all kinds of watches. Only certain ones would stand bridge watches, but there was communications, and engineering, and gunnery, and the ship's organization officers like damage control, fire control. It requires a great many officers, and you see, also we carried two 50-foot tank lighters, and 28 of the 36-foot landing boats, and then we also had two smaller boats, like scouting boats. Our boat division required lots of personnel. It would take three men just for the crew of each boat and an officer in charge.

Peter Spectre: So the men assigned to your ship weren't just to operate the ship, but to operate the boats that the ship carried.

Admiral O'Neill: That's right. That's what we called the boat division.

Peter Spectre: What did they do when they weren't landing?

Admiral O'Neill: Well, we were drilling, and watch standing, and in the morning and night we had general quarters. Everyone had to go to his battle station. In the morning, for example, we'd sound GQ, as we called it, 30 or 45 minutes before daylight, and you'd have to stand there until well after daylight and man your station, all the guns. Then at nighttime, the same thing; you had to go to general quarters before sunset until well after sunset. And there was lots of drilling going on all day long.

Peter Spectre: How much time did you have to train before you began the voyage to North Africa?

Admiral O'Neill: They had been training at Cove Point several times before I joined the ship. We made one what we called a dress-rehearsal run, after I joined. Then, when we came back from the North African landing, we began training for the Sicily landing. We made many trips up there. Load the troops and take them up for two or three days and send them ashore, and bring them back aboard, take them down to Norfolk, and then get ready for another group to take up to Cove Point.

Peter Spectre: In other words, you didn't just train with the people who were going to go across with you?

Admiral O'Neill: Our own boat crews had to be trained.

Peter Spectre: You weren't carrying troops when you were practicing up at Cove Point?

Admiral O'Neill: Oh, yes, the whole works. Our men were training at the same time. In other words, the lowering of the boats, the hoisting of the boats. They were getting great experience at that. And the men handling the cargo booms—the fictitious cargo. We had pine logs that we loaded in the hold of the ship to represent shells and ammunition—all kinds of fake things like that that had to be hoisted out of the hold and lowered into the boats after the troops. You'd send the troops in first, and then the boats came back, and you loaded ammunition and water, medical supplies, small tanks, vehicles, bulldozers, and everything had to be pub in the boats and sent ashore. Then what they did ashore, I don't know. Then it all had to be brought back, and all that stuff had to be loaded back in the hold of the ship and the crew and troops brought back aboard. And then, the following morning, we'd do it all over again. It was quite a rigmarole.

Peter Spectre: Were there other transports with you? So what you were doing was conducting the North Africa invasion in Chesapeake Bay?

Admiral O'Neill: Yes, exactly. We were making the North African landings right up here at Cove Point. At one time there were about 15 or 20 transports. Then we had these small lighters, these LCTs that carried the heavy equipment ashore, like the big tanks. The heavy tanks were carried up on the cargo ships, what we called the AKs.

Peter Spectre: How many ships went across to Africa? Did you steam in a squadron.

Admiral O'Neill: Oh, yes. It was a very large convoy. I think out of Norfolk there were about 15, but we were joined by other ships from other ports along the coast to meet up with us out at sea. So by the time the entire convoy was assembled, it looked like the whole ocean was full of ships. The total number there, I have no idea, because that's not only the transports and cargo ships but also the escorts, the flagships, and all. The escorts and the screens, they call it, too. There were a great many Navy destroyers, battleships, everywhere. The whole ocean was covered.

Peter Spectre: This was the first U.S. invasion during the war?

Admiral O'Neill: It was the first in the Atlantic, but I think maybe the first was down in the South Pacific. I believe down in Guadalcanal was the first.* I wasn't there.

---

* On 7 August 1942, U.S. Marines invaded the islands of Guadalcanal and Tulagi in the Solomons chain as part of the first U.S. counteroffensive in the Pacific War. The primary purpose was to gain control of an airstrip on Guadalcanal and thus to prevent the Japanese from achieving control of the surrounding air and sea regions. The campaign was long and difficult before organized Japanese resistance finally ended on 9 February 1943.

Peter Spectre: You had never had any experience in a convoy before this point?

Admiral O'Neill: No.

Peter Spectre: What was it like? Did you have any troubles?

Admiral O'Neill: Well, as I say, I was fortunate in having a number of officers aboard who had been on these expeditions when the ship was just a troop carrier. They'd had some convoy experience and were familiar with the zigzag patterns. We also carried the Navy staff, the amphibious force commander, aboard ship.* Then, later on, after that operation, the division commander stayed aboard and eventually went with us to the Pacific. But what we're talking about now is the North African invasion.

Peter Spectre: What happened when you arrived at the beaches in North Africa?

Admiral O'Neill: We landed at a small place called Fedhala, and unfortunately there was heavy surf. The ships were to land about daylight, and most of the transports lost most of their small boats. The troops could get in to the beach. The boats could drop their ramps, and the troops could get out and wade ashore. And before the boats could back off, the surf would throw this boat back up on the beach, and we lost practically all of our boats in the landing.

Peter Spectre: Did you get all the men ashore, though?

Admiral O'Neill: Oh yes, we got the men ashore, but we had no salvage equipment, none of the ships. There were many ships around there, and they all lost most of their boats. We weren't the only one. But there was no salvage equipment, no tug or anything to come up and yank the things off the beach. I think it was the first night in there, when the German sub got in there and sank two of the transports and a destroyer, maybe three

---

* Captain Robert R. M. Emmet, USN, commanded the center attack group transports.

transports.* We got under way and went to sea to get away from the sub so we could go out and zigzag and get the screening up to protect us. Then we came back into the harbor of Casablanca so we could unload the supplies. We couldn't unload our equipment and supplies, because we had no boats and the surf was up there. The landing was in terrible condition.

Peter Spectre: Your original intent was to land the supplies with men?

Admiral O'Neill: So we had to go in the harbor, alongside the pier, and unload and dump the stuff out on the pier. Then the Army had to take over and haul it to wherever they needed it.

Peter Spectre: It was lucky that we had Casablanca.

Admiral O'Neill: Yes. By that time it had been subdued. The resistance wasn't too much there. The French put up some resistance in the beginning, but it didn't amount to much.

There's an interesting story there. I don't know all the details of it, but aboard our ship we carried an Army officer, a colonel, who had attended a French military academy with some of these French officers that were in command of the French forces there. They had been close personal friends. He had a secret letter that he carried inside his pocket. He told me about it; I didn't see it. He was the first one to be put ashore in a boat with a Jeep. He was to fly this French flag and this American flag on the Jeep and get into contact with these several French officers to make sure they would tell their forces to not put up any resistance. How well that worked, I don't know. Apparently it worked to some extent, because the resistance was very mild and casualties very few.

Of course, before that there had been some diplomatic maneuvering going on. I think there was a man by the name of Murphy.† He was supposed to have contacted the French forces, and we had orders that if the French searchlights on shore were showing

---

* For details on the ship losses, see Morison, Volume II, pages 283-294.
† Robert D. Murphy, counselor of the American Embassy at Vichy, France. See Rick Atkinson, *An Army at Dawn: the War in North Africa, 1942-1943* (New York: Henry Holt & Co., 2002).

straight up to the sky, then they would offer no resistance. When we went in there, as we approached, they could hear us, I guess, or maybe saw us with their radar, and the searchlights began pointing straight up. So that was fine. Just a few minutes later, the lights lowered and shone right on us and started shooting. There was a little gunfire back and forth between some of the shore batteries and the destroyers that were protecting us, but it didn't amount to too much.

Peter Spectre: How long were you there before you made the return trip?

Admiral O'Neill: We were there, I guess, altogether, about three days. Because as soon as we unloaded at Casablanca we got out of there. Formed up the convoy offshore and came on back to Norfolk.

Peter Spectre: Was there any provision made for re-embarking the troops in case they were forced back? Was that ever considered?

Admiral O'Neill: If it was, we weren't informed of it. I suppose they had some evacuation plan, the Dunkirk idea, but if they did, no one knew about it.[*]

Peter Spectre: Your understanding was that you were to leave the goods and the troops?

Admiral O'Neill: And then it was up to them to carry on from there.

Peter Spectre: Anything else that happened then that you could remember that was significant?

Admiral O'Neill: No, I don't know. The first morning, while we were anchored there off Fedhala, just shortly north of Casablanca, some of the French light cruisers and

---

[*] As France neared defeat at the hands of Germany in the spring of 1940, a collection of small British naval vessels and private craft evacuated 338,226 British, French, and Belgian soldiers and delivered them safely to Britain. The operation, which took place in and near the English Channel port of Dunkirk, France, lasted from 26 May to 4 June.

destroyers came out and began firing at our transport ships, and also there was a French battleship in there called the *Jean Bart*. She was one of the big ones with 15-inch guns, but she could only use the forward turret. I think there were three guns in the turret. And she got into a little gun duel with the *Augusta*, a heavy cruiser, and the *Brooklyn*, a light cruiser. It was a very pretty picture to stand there on the deck of the transport and watch this gun duel between these ships.

Actually, they sortied from Casablanca with the idea of sinking the transports, but fortunately we had the battleship *Massachusetts* down the coastline so she could silence the guns of the *Jean Bart*. They were about the same size battleships, and then we had the cruiser *Augusta* and the cruiser *Brooklyn* to stay right close to the transports. The *Massachusetts* was way off below the horizon. But it was a very pretty picture to see this. These shells all had dye in them, and when they hit it would be a big purple splash, and another one would be yellow, and another one would be green. They did that to aid the spotters aboard the ship to change the range and so forth. But, other than that, it was more or less routine. The tragic thing was that we lost most of our boats.

Peter Spectre: What did you learn from your first invasion experience? You conducted quite a few after that.

Admiral O'Neill: Well, we learned many things. I think our boat crews gained a lot of experience landing in the surf. The entire ship's organization was strengthened a little bit, because the best way to learn is when you're actually under fire and experiencing the things that don't come up in a rehearsal like at Cove Point. It was excellent training for the officers and the cargo-handling crew, of getting the cargo unloaded.

Peter Spectre: What was your responsibility? Where did your responsibility to the troops end? Your job was strictly to get them on the shore, and that was it?

Admiral O'Neill: To land them at H-hour and then get their supplies and equipment ashore as quickly as possible in the order in which they wanted it. Now, that had to be done this way. When the ship loaded the cargo supplies, say, at Norfolk, it was loaded with the idea that the equipment that they wanted first would naturally be on top, and that worked quite well. There were times, also, when we'd get a call back from the beach, and they would want certain things that weren't right there next to go. So we would have to haul those up and pile them over on the deck someplace and go down and get the equipment that they needed ashore. That was the important thing, to give them what they wanted. But that was our primary responsibility—land them safely and unload the gear.

Peter Spectre: Did you personally direct the disembarkation of the troops and supplies?

Admiral O'Neill: That was all organization. Men had certain jobs assigned. We had officers down supervising the unloading of the forward holds, also officers back supervising unloading aft. I didn't personally supervise it.

Peter Spectre: Who coordinated all the transports? Whom did you get your orders from?

Admiral O'Neill: Our task force commander.

Peter Spectre: You were always in touch with him?

Admiral O'Neill: Oh, yes. Then, of course, the overall commander of the entire expedition—he's the one who sets the H-hour and decides when to start and the area where we were to anchor. We didn't actually anchor. We stopped, and we dropped the anchor what we call underfoot—just to hold us there in position with the ship ready to move any time, full watches on—engine room, bridge, everywhere.

Peter Spectre: You went back to Norfolk. What happened then?

Admiral O'Neill: Well, we went back to Norfolk, and we had a few weeks to remove a lot of the wooden paneling and furniture and things that were a fire hazard. Then got ready to load troops, and we started in rehearsing in January. We got back the end of November. We were there, I think, the month of December in Norfolk. Then we started loading troops and made our first run up in Cove Point in January in bitter cold weather, and we rehearsed there until we got ready for the next operation, which was to be Sicily.

Peter Spectre: Did you know what you were training for? Did you have any idea where you were going?

Admiral O'Neill: No. The first time we got a lot of information, the North African expedition, we got a lot of that from newspapermen ashore there in Norfolk. But the Sicily invasion, we had no idea. We could all second-guess. There was a lot of talk among us aboard the ship as to where we thought we were going next. We didn't make very good guesses, but we opened our orders after we got to sea. We started with the officers and the coxswains of the boats. We had maps showing the coast of Sicily, where we were to land. The Army had made up these tables, topographical—made out of plaster of Paris—showing the beaches and the creeks and the hills and where the trees were located. All that had been obtained long before by the Army. Then we had meetings every day all the way across with the key men that were going to land so they would have some idea what it would look like. And we trained with our gun crews and stood regular watches. The most difficult part of it was this rehearsal off Cove Point in January and February. As you well know, it's rugged.

Peter Spectre: By this time you probably had quite a bit of experience dealing with the Navy, since you really were in the Navy at that time, and in the Army to a certain extent. How was your relationship?

Admiral O'Neill: Very good, very pleasant.

Peter Spectre: How did Navy men look at you as Coast Guard?

Admiral O'Neill: I think most of them had a fairly high regard for the officers and the men. A great many of the Navy personnel were reserve officers, like many of ours were. They'd been through OCS, and so had ours, and they got along fine. The fact that we were flagship for—it was the division commander who kept us on our toes all the time, because he wanted a good job done.

Peter Spectre: Who was it?

Admiral O'Neill: For the North African landing it was Captain Emmet. Then he was relieved at the end of that by Captain Phillips, and he was our division commander for the Sicily operation that we began to rehearse for in Chesapeake Bay, and during the Sicily operation.[*] He was relieved later by another man after we got into the Pacific.

Peter Spectre: Why don't we talk a little bit about the Sicily campaign? You trained at Cove Point again? When did you leave for Sicily?

Admiral O'Neill: I think early in June we left.[†] That would have to be verified. We spent all that time training and rehearsing. That was another large convoy. The trip across for the Sicily landing was very similar to the trip for the North African landing. So much had to be done aboard ship. We had these conferences on what to do and when to do it and what to expect and do everything we possibly could to get ready for every eventuality that we could think of.

Peter Spectre: It must have been very difficult to keep track of all these things.

Admiral O'Neill: Well, it required a big organization and lots of people to help run it. That's why we had so many officers and so many men, because every man had a job. Every man and every officer had an important job to do—whether it was the cook in the galley, or the gunnery officer, or fire control officer, damage control group, the boat division, the cargo-handling crew. Every man had a very important job.

Peter Spectre: What were the troops doing when you were crossing?

---

[*] Captain Wallace B. Phillips, USN, Commander Transport Division One.
[†] The *Leonard Wood* left Norfolk 3 June 1943 and arrived in the port of Mers el-Kébir, Algeria, on 22 June.

Admiral O'Neill: I think they were just loafing around and resting. I do know the officers held numerous meetings with them. They would gather down on the forecastle deck, large groups at a time, and they would be talked to by their officers, but what it was all about, I don't know. I could see them down there. Of course, at nighttime, the ship always at sea, had to be darkened, and no smoking allowed above deck, no lights could show. They weren't supposed to show. Every once in a while somebody would make a mistake and, not thinking, light a cigarette out on deck. That always stirred up a little confusion for a few minutes.

Peter Spectre: How many soldiers did you carry?

Admiral O'Neill: I think we carried 1,700; they were combat troops.

Peter Spectre: Did you have any problems with submarines going across?

Admiral O'Neill: No. The German submarines, so-called wolf packs, were following us all the time, but our screen was so heavy and so efficient that they kept them away from us. We didn't lose a ship going across the Atlantic either time. The only time a submarine hit us was there off North Africa when they got inside the screen some way and sank, I think, three transports before we could get out of there and get away from them. At sea there was no real danger. We were not really concerned at all, because we had the most efficient screen I've ever seen. Destroyers everywhere—ahead of us, behind us.

Peter Spectre: Were Coast Guard cutters involved?

Admiral O'Neill: No. The Coast Guard cutters were used later on in the Atlantic. All during the war I think they were with the troop carriers, not with the amphibious forces.

Peter Spectre: Tell me a little bit about the landing at Sicily.

Admiral O'Neill: The landing at Sicily was at a little Italian town there called Scoglitti.* We had no great trouble except right at the very beginning. When we first anchored there, the Germans found out about it, and they dropped flares over our head there and illuminated the entire area, many square miles of these very efficient flares. I guess they were the magnesium flares. Then they started dropping bombs after the area was illuminated, and a destroyer was hit and sunk and lost with all hands right astern of us.† We were fortunate on that.

Our gunnery officer, who is now the district commander in Norfolk, did an excellent job, because as soon as the planes would approach, he would fire all of our antiaircraft guns just to put up a screen, and I think that was very effective in keeping the planes from coming directly over us with their bombs.‡ There were several losses there of ships but not heavy.

There was one unfortunate thing that happened there. I don't know the details on it, but I do know that there were paratroopers that were being brought in, and apparently somebody mistook them for enemy planes and shot down some of them. One of our boats coming back from the beach picked up one of the pilots from one of these planes, and he said he was shot down by one of our own people. That's an accident that happens in all engagements. It's happening over in Vietnam right today. Losses of that type were not heavy. I don't know how many planes were shot down by mistake, very few. But we do know of this one, because we picked the pilot up.

Peter Spectre: He must have been hopping mad.

Admiral O'Neill: I guess he was. Anyway, the landing went along smoothly, and we got all the troops ashore and all the equipment ashore. We lost no boats. I guess we were there about 36 hours.

---

* The invasion began on the morning of 10 July 1943.
† Bombs fell near the destroyer *Tillman* (DD-641) and temporarily knocked out her surface-search radar, but she was not otherwise damaged.
‡ Rear Admiral Edward C. Allen, Jr., USCG, commanded the Fifth Coast Guard District in 1970. During his time on board the *Leonard Wood* he was a lieutenant and lieutenant commander.

The Army made good progress ashore. They were well supported by good gunfire from the Navy ships, cruisers and destroyers. They helped to subdue some of the German tanks that were heading for the beach. Then there was a small British ship. She looked something like the *Monitor* in Civil War days. She had one big 15-inch turret up forward, and she was firing that over our heads, which was interesting for a while.* But everything went along smoothly.

Prior to our landing, we went into Mers el-Kébir, the seaport of Oran, and we rehearsed at a beach near there for the actual landing on the coast of Sicily. After the landing, we came back to Mers el-Kébir and took aboard 800 German officers of Rommel's army as prisoners.† They were all ranks from colonel on down to what we would call a lieutenant. We took them aboard, and other ships loaded prisoners, mostly the enlisted. I think we carried most of the officers and brought them back to Norfolk. We went into the Army disembarkation pier, and they were loaded aboard passenger trains. Some were hauled down into Virginia and kept down there until the war was over, and then we sent them home.

We had no trouble coming home with them. We kept about half of them forward in the troops' compartments, which were all empty, of course; the other half was back aft. We'd not let any of our people down below deck except the chaplain and one of our doctors went down occasionally to confer with the German doctors. There were two German doctors with them. One German doctor asked for a conference with our doctor, because some of his men had a disease that he couldn't diagnose. We have seven doctors aboard, and they finally discovered it to be what they called Weil's disease, a liver ailment and apparently contagious, but it didn't spread, so nothing terrible happened on that.

The prisoners were well fed. We fed them twice a day. Our mess boys would carry food down to the hatch, and their mess attendants would come up and get these huge cans of soup and stew or whatever they were fed. They were well fed.

---

* This ship was the monitor HMS *Abercrombie*, which had gone into service with the Royal Navy in 1941. She looked like a truncated battleship with one two-gun 15-inch turret forward of the superstructure.

† Erwin Rommel, known as "The Desert Fox," was a German field marshal in World War II. He led the German campaign in North Africa and later in the defense of France against Allied invasion. He was forced by Hitler to commit suicide in 1944.

We had guards there on the lower bridge to make sure they didn't come storming out of there and try to take over the ship. We would let maybe 75 come up on deck certain times during the day for fresh air and exercise, and the senior colonel with the German prisoners sent a letter up to me by way of the chaplain, and he complained that we were violating the provisions of the Geneva Convention—that they rated better quarters. We paid no attention to that, because we knew that they were comfortable as we could make them. They were well fed, plenty of fresh water to drink, they could take baths with seawater the same as our troops did. We didn't feel sorrowful about that, but I guess he wanted to complain about something. Maybe he wanted to take over the captain's cabin, I don't know. But that was minor. That's just a sidelight.

Interview Number 3 with Admiral Merlin O'Neill, U.S. Coast Guard (Retired)
Place: Admiral O'Neill's home in Lusby, Maryland
Date: Saturday, 25 April 1970
Interviewer: Peter Spectre

Peter Spectre: Admiral, the last time we had an interview we talked about the Sicily invasion, and we left off where you had just come back from the Sicily invasion, and you had unloaded your prisoners and were beginning your next tour. Carry on from there, please.

Admiral O'Neill: After unloading our German officers from Rommel's Afrika Korps onto passenger trains at the Army port of embarkation at Newport News, we prepared then for a trip around to the Pacific with Pearl Harbor as our destination.

Peter Spectre: This was still on the *Leonard Wood*?

Admiral O'Neill: On the *Leonard Wood*. This was the later part of November or early December; we sailed from Norfolk. Down at the Panama Canal we took about 2,500 Army troops just as straight transport to take them to Honolulu.

Peter Spectre: Do you know where they were from?

Admiral O'Neill: I think they were from the Seventh Division, as I recall.

Peter Spectre: Were you traveling in a convoy or by yourself?

Admiral O'Neill: We were traveling alone then.

Peter Spectre: Did you have any escort?

Admiral O'Neill: No, we had no escorts. We did our own zigzagging during daylight hours. Then we stopped at San Francisco for fuel, water, and supplies and sailed along to Honolulu. We had to put in at the city of Honolulu, because at that time there was no berthing space available for us at Pearl.[*] We were there just a few days and then went around to Pearl and began rehearsing for the Gilbert Islands operation.

Peter Spectre: Did you know when you left the East Coast for Hawaii what operations you were going to be involved in?

Admiral O'Neill: We didn't know for sure, but what little information we gathered now and then from talk among the officers and certain bits of correspondence, it appeared that this sort of island-hopping operation would start in the Gilberts and move to the Marshall Islands. That was guesswork but a pretty good guess, as is later turned out.

Peter Spectre: Was this island-hopping policy one that was explained to everybody? Was it strategy that was understood by everyone?

Admiral O'Neill: It was strategy that was understood by everyone that that was to be the approach to Japan—from island to island. It later on turned out that some of the islands were bypassed; it wasn't to take every island you came to. Actually, that's what it developed into. One of our dress rehearsals there at an uninhabited island in the Hawaii chain was on Christmas Eve. It was a full dress rehearsal with the support ships and the planes and all, and the landings with the troops in the boats took place on Christmas morning. It was not a particularly happy Christmas for any of us. Then we went back to Pearl and in a few days sailed for the Gilbert Islands. After we got to sea, it was common knowledge that the island where we would make our landings, the division that I was in, was the Makin Island.[†] Others went to other islands in the Gilbert group.

---

[*] The *Leonard Wood* arrived at Honolulu on 27 September 1943.
[†] The *Leonard Wood* participated in the amphibious assault on Makin Island on 19 November 1943. The rehearsal that Admiral O'Neill recalled occurring on Christmas was probably for the Marshall Islands operation in early 1944.

Peter Spectre: The type of landings that you did in the Atlantic you practiced for in the Chesapeake Bay, and what you actually did in North Africa and Sicily were on different types of beaches than what you would encounter in the South Pacific. Were you aware of that when you did your practice landings? Did you take into account that there was going to be different types of conditions?

Admiral O'Neill: Yes, very definitely. The landings in the islands in the Gilbert and Marshall groups were coral. There were coral sand and coral reefs to get through, and it all depended on which beach they picked out for ships. They usually referred to them by color—red beach, blue beach, yellow beach, and sometimes on some of the beaches the boats would have to go in almost in single file in order to get through an opening in the coral reef to getup to the beach itself, which was almost in all cases coral sand. As it turned out, the opposition at Makin was not nearly as heavy as some of the other Gilbert landings. There was opposition and casualties, but not nearly as heavy as like at Tarawa, for example.[*]

Peter Spectre: How many other ships were in the task force?

Admiral O'Neill: In our particular division, there were five. There were three transports and two cargo ships.

Peter Spectre: These were just going to Makin?

Admiral O'Neill: Yes. Of course, each task group had their own support ships and planes assigned them to protect them. After landing at Makin—it was several days involved there. At the end of the day we usually got under way and stood out to sea, and the groups would form up out there under escort to get away from submarine dangers and enemy bombing at night.

---

[*] U.S. Marines, supported by warships of the Central Pacific Force, invaded Tarawa on 20 November 1943 to begin the capture of the Gilbert Islands. The Japanese provided stiff, deadly resistance.

Peter Spectre: Were there any Japanese ships in the area?

Admiral O'Neill: No Japanese ships. There were planes and submarines. It was at the Makin landing when the small aircraft carrier, the *Liscome Bay*, was torpedoed.[*] She was in another group. We were about five or six miles from her, and we saw her when she was hit. It was late at night or early morning. Then the destroyers and other ships in the area picked up survivors, and later on these survivors were transferred to us. When our duties were all over, the troops had been landed, the supplies had been put ashore, we took aboard the survivors and returned them to Pearl Harbor. Many of them were burn cases, and I think we carried about 200 or 250. Out there in the Pacific at that time there were no Navy hospital ships, and in view of the fact that we had a good-size sick bay, hospital, and we carried seven doctors and quite a few corpsmen, we functioned there at the end of the operation as a hospital ship. We took aboard the casualties from Makin. They were all brought aboard our ship.

Admiral O'Neill: These include soldiers from the beach as well as survivors?

Admiral O'Neill: Yes. And we also brought aboard a group of prisoners. The coxswain of one of our landing craft brought aboard about 50 prisoners, and everybody thought they were Japanese. We sent over to the flagship for an Army intelligence officer, and he came over and identified them immediately by language and appearance as Korean. The Japs had brought down many Koreans out of the islands as laborers. They weren't soldiers; they were something like our Seabees, just common laborers.[†] We brought the whole group back to Pearl, and then we began getting ready for the next landing, which tuned out to be the Marshall Islands.

Peter Spectre: Were there any other Coast Guard-manned ships with you?

---

[*] The escort carrier *Liscome Bay* (CVE-56) was torpedoed and sunk by the Japanese submarine *I-175* on the morning of 24 November 1943 while supporting the invasion of the Gilbert Islands. Of those on board, 624 were lost and 272 were rescued. Among those killed was Rear Admiral Henry M. Mullinnix, USN, embarked as Commander Task Group 52.3.
[†] Seabees is the nickname applied to members of the Navy's mobile construction battalions (CBs).

Admiral O'Neill: Yes, there were two transports and one cargo ship which were Navy, manned by Coast Guard. Then our next operation, I think, was in February of '44. We carried the reserve troops; other transports carried the assault troops. But we carried the reserve regiment to go ashore if they needed them. Kwajalein was the name of the island.[*]

Peter Spectre: Did you have any opposition there?

Admiral O'Neill: There was no opposition on land. We were inside the lagoon, and there were no submarines in there and no planes. Going through the entrance to the lagoon, we steamed through there in column formation, in daylight, and there was an island on our port hand called Perry Island. You could have thrown a lead line over to the island, it was so close.[†] And later on it turned out that there were about 1,200 Jap troops on the island. They were hiding in their bunkers and pillboxes, and they had to be subdued by Army troops and Marines later on.

Peter Spectre: They didn't bother you?

Admiral O'Neill: No, nobody saw anything. While we were in the lagoon there, anchored, after Kwajalein had been taken, we prepared for Eniwetok, which is up at the north end of the lagoon.[‡]

Peter Spectre: You didn't go back and get supplies? You stayed right there?

Admiral O'Neill: We stayed right there. We carried Marines that time, up to Eniwetok. I don't remember the date of the landing up there, but it had been shelled and bombed heavily; there was opposition ashore.

---

[*] U.S. troops invaded Kwajalein Atoll in the western Marshall Islands on 1 February 1944. Kwajalein fell on 6 February, and the entire atoll was declared secured.
[†] One method of measuring depth of water is to cast a line into the water; the line is weighted on the end with a piece of lead.
[‡] U.S. amphibious forces invaded Eniwetok Atoll in the Marshall Islands on 17 February 1944.

I noticed the Marine Corps had a system where they used equipment like machine guns on bicycle wheels, and we unloaded equipment like that for them. It was interesting how they just spread out all over the island very quickly; they just overran the island and kept a lot of the Japs in their bunkers and pillboxes. The Navy had two of the old battleships, and they would blow up these Jap bunkers. They were built with thick walls of concrete, and their piercing shells were ideal for blowing up Jap bunkers and destroying them that way. It was an interesting show, and we used to watch the shells from these battleships when they'd fire them. You could see the projectiles going through the air, almost a flat trajectory.

Peter Spectre: Did you have any difficulty maneuvering around these islands? Was there information about the conditions?

Admiral O'Neill: Much of the information came from the British. They had used freighters and trading ships through there and done quite a bit of surveying locally, and many of our charts came from that source. We also had aboard a British officer who was familiar with those islands. He'd been out there many times in his career, and he was a great help to us in avoiding any pitfalls or landing on the coral reef. The charts were really very good, and another thing—that territory and shoreline had been photographed before we went out there by the Navy from a submarine, and also some aerial pictures. The only opposition that we had there at Eniwetok was some Jap planes came over a few times at night from the Truk Islands, further to the northwest. But they did no damage. The opposition was principally on shore.

Peter Spectre: Did you know what was happening to the major fleets, the Japanese war fleet and our war fleet? Did you know that you were safe from a Japanese fleet coming down and disturbing the operation?

Admiral O'Neill: No, we didn't know it. We saw none of the major units of the Navy. We figured that they were busy on other things, particularly with the main Jap fleet. The Jap planes were very active. They still had many of their expert pilots, and lost a lot of them later on, as history tells us. There were two of the light aircraft carriers in addition to the *Liscome Bay*.[*] They were our air protection. They didn't carry many planes, but they were suitable for the amphibious work. They were assigned to this amphibious force.

Peter Spectre: We've talked about a lot of amphibious invasions so far, and we've never really talked about how these were organized. How was this whole thing organized? You had more than one ship involved, thousands of men involved. What did you do before these invasions took place?

Admiral O'Neill: Well, the ships that were to make up a division would be, say, three or four transports and one or two cargo ships. They would be assigned; that would be just one unit of the entire amphibious force. Then the troops that we were to carry would be assigned by the Army or the Marine Corps—the number and the unit, the battalion or the regiment, or whatever it may be. Then it was up to the Army to provide the supplies and material, the ammunition, guns and tanks, and all that equipment that had to be sent ashore. Then the date was set for us to take aboard the units that were assigned to our different transports for rehearsal.

Then the rehearsal area would be picked out by our authority long before. We had our own organization aboard. For example, our boat division and the troops had to be rehearsed as to where to go before the landing actually took place so that when the rehearsal started, the troop officers would know where to bring their squads and their platoons to a certain place aboard ship and get aboard that boat when the order was given.

Peter Spectre: Who figured all this out?

Admiral O'Neill: It was a combination of Navy, Army, Marine Corps, Coast Guard—a group would get together and plan, and it would be passed down the line to the lower echelon. It sounds highly complicated, and it actually was, but all these different units

---

[*] The escort carriers that supported the Eniwetok group in which the *Leonard Wood* operated with the *Nassau* (CVE-16) and the *Natoma Bay* (CVE-62).

and groups of people meeting at a conference and coordinating all these different activities of men and supplies. For example, aboard ship we had to look out for our own supplies, food and water, and training our boat crews. Then it all dovetailed and worked in together when we started rehearsing. In the rehearsals we ironed out a lot of the bugs so that the operation would be smooth when we actually landed on an enemy beach.

Peter Spectre: As an example, say that you had a group of Army troops that were going to come to your transport, and they wanted to bring equipment with them. How did you avoid having them bring too much equipment with them that wouldn't fit in your ship?

Admiral O'Neill: That was done by the Army. The Army had an embarkation officer assigned, and he knew exactly the size of the hold of the ship. He knew exactly the bulk capacity, the carrying capacity, how many troops we could carry. He handled all that. The actual equipment that the troops brought was just light equipment for their own use—their rifles and canteens and things like that. The heavy equipment was all laid out by the Army and loaded according to a schedule that they wanted. The first things they wanted to be put on shore were loaded on top, so they had to go into the hold last. We always carried a few Army and Marine Corps officers to supervise that, and it was up to us to load it and unload it according to the plans that they worked out.

Peter Spectre: It sounds really confusing.

Admiral O'Neill: It was, but with frequent conferences—you see, we had conferences on board ship every day and sometimes all day long with our boat division officer, the troop officers, the lieutenants, the captains, the majors, the lieutenant colonels and all of them down the line. It took a lot of time to work those things out, but time was not of the essence in all those cases; they were all planned well ahead. The only operation that hadn't been planned way ahead was at Eniwetok when we just went from one island to the other.

Most of those exercises, after the first one, our crew was well schooled on those operations as to what other people were supposed to do, as well as what they themselves were supposed to do, and they were all old-timers, so to speak. I think that made it a lot easier for a new group of Army men or Marine Corps people to come aboard and work with our people, because our people could help them and give them advice on the loading, the training of the troops, the assembling, and all. The Marine Corps officers were more familiar with the ship and shipboard routine, Navy routine, and Navy regulations, so it was a lot easier for them and easier for us to work with them, because they were all part of the family. Everybody got along all right, but sometimes the Army would send a group of young officers aboard, and the ship was a strange vehicle to them. It took them a little while to become accustomed to routine, what the ship looked like, and how to find their way around aboard ship.

Peter Spectre: What happened after the landing at Eniwetok?

Admiral O'Neill: After Eniwetok we came back to Pearl and discharged our few troops we had left aboard, and then we were supposed to get ready for another operation in the Pacific. Our orders were changed, and they said we were to go to California, to the naval shipyard at the Los Angeles port. So we set sail alone, without escort, from Pearl Harbor to Los Angeles. We went into the shipyard there for what we call the availability, and I think the ship was there for about six weeks.

Peter Spectre: Was the purpose overhaul?

Admiral O'Neill: It was general overhaul. The ship had had no overhaul for many months, and she'd done a great deal of cruising. The engines and boilers needed care and cleaning, overhaul repairing. Then, shortly after we arrived there, I got orders transferring me to headquarters in Washington to await further orders. I was told those further orders would be to a transport to haul troops from, say, the East Coast to England and France, getting ready for the big show in France. I reported to headquarters and—

Peter Spectre: Did you want to leave the *Leonard Wood*?

Admiral O'Neill: Not particularly. I had a good crew and a good ship, and I assumed that I would be on there until the end of the war. That was perfectly satisfactory with me. When we first arrived at Long Beach, we were told that we could grant leave to our officers and men on a rotation basis, so about half the officers aboard went on leave for about a week. Then it was my turn. My family, Esther and Patricia and Marilyn, were living in Norfolk, so I hopped aboard a transport plane and flew to Norfolk for a week and flew back to Long Beach to rejoin my ship. I was glad to see my family, but it was wartime, and I expected to go to sea. I'd been at sea for 18 months, and I flew back, and then after I got out there, they said my orders had been changed, and I was to be transferred to the Marine Corps base at Quantico.[*]

Peter Spectre: You told me before that when you were on the *Leonard Wood* you only had one casualty the whole period of time that you were on it.

Admiral O'Neill: Yes. That was at the Makin Island operation—our only casualty. We had the 36-foot landing boats—we called them LCVPs—that carried two .30-caliber machine guns in rings just forward of the coxswain. After the boat had discharged the troops, a member of the boat crew fell and discharged the gun in falling. It fired one shot, and it killed him instantly. That was our only casualty any time any time that I was aboard the ship.

Peter Spectre: That was really tragic, especially after having such good luck for such a long period of time.

Admiral O'Neill: To be killed in an accident like that.

Peter Spectre: Now we'll go back to where you were directed, to Quantico.

---

[*] Quantico, Virginia, which is on the Potomac River south of Washington, D.C., is the site of a Marine Corps base.

Admiral O'Neill: I was supposed to go down there and take charge of the training of beach parties. Those were the men who went on shore to handle the traffic, so to speak.

Peter Spectre: These were Navy men?

Admiral O'Neill: These were Coast Guard men. I reported down there, and I was there about ten days or two weeks and relieved the officer there. Then I received orders to report to the Commandant of the Coast Guard the following morning at 8:00 o'clock. Well, there were no planes that I could commandeer to fly me to headquarters, so I got one of the men from the base, stationed in the Coast Guard group there, to drive me up to Washington. We drove all night long. I got up there and reported to the Commandant, and he said, "We're transferring you to Baltimore, in charge of the Baltimore section. That would be called Pier Four, the shore patrol, port security, training station for training firefighters, small-boat repair yard, and merchant marine safety. All those small units constituted the Baltimore section.

Peter Spectre: Why did you receive that assignment?

Peter Spectre: I don't know why they picked me. I was very happy down at Quantico. I had just gotten there and gotten started. I can't answer that.

Peter Spectre: What were your feelings about it, especially in light of the fact you thought that you were going to a transport that was going to Europe?

Admiral O'Neill: First I didn't go on a transport to Europe; that was apparently somebody's idea. I don't think it was ever very serious, because I was picked for this Quantico job instead. I wasn't particularly happy about being transferred from Quantico to Baltimore, because my family would have been able to come to Quantico; we would have had quarters. As a matter of fact, the quarters that were assigned to me were vacant and ready to move into, and I had told my wife and daughters to get ready to move. We had actually started to contact the moving companies to move us from Norfolk to

Quantico when, all of a sudden, out of the clear blue sky, came this order. Anyway, it came about and worked out very well.

I was there in Baltimore for about six months. Then I was transferred back to headquarters and assigned as assistant finance and supply officer. I knew nothing about finance and supply; that hadn't been my business during the war or any time during my service. Anyway, I was there for a short time, and then I received orders to go to Norfolk as the district commander. At that time I held the exalted rank of commodore.

Peter Spectre: You got promoted before you went to Norfolk?

Admiral O'Neill: When I got to Norfolk.

Peter Spectre: How many commodores were there in the Coast Guard?

Admiral O'Neill: There were several. That was a wartime rank. The Army had a one-star officer known as a brigadier general, and in order to have a comparable rank in the Navy they reinstituted the rank of commodore, which was one star. Then we followed the Navy, because we were in the Navy then. Some of our officers were appointed. I don't know the exact number, but there were several.

Peter Spectre: Why is it that commodores don't exist? The Army has always had brigadier generals?

Admiral O'Neill: I think the Navy and the Coast Guard figured that there's no particular need for a rank between a captain and a rear admiral. We don't need a brigade commander, because the captain's duties and the rear admiral's duties are close, and the rung on the ladder from captain to rear admiral is a very short one.

Then I went to Norfolk and moved my family after the short tour of duty in finance and supply.

Peter Spectre: Did you move your family from Baltimore to Washington to Norfolk?

Admiral O'Neill: That's right. I moved the family back down to Norfolk, and in those days housing was hard to find, but we managed each time to find a place. When my family first moved to Norfolk, I was at sea. Esther put our furniture in storage in Washington, and she moved down to Norfolk and stayed with a friend. She was supposed to get a house that was to be vacated by a Coast Guard officer as soon as he got orders. All of a sudden, someone at Coast Guard Headquarters shipped our furniture to Norfolk, and here the furniture was sitting in a van and no place to put it. She called the personnel officer on the phone at headquarters and said, "This furniture's been sitting out here all day long. I didn't ask for it. The driver told me it's costing the government ten dollars an hour to keep the furniture there." This other officer was awaiting orders, and in an hour or two he got his orders to move out. So, as his furniture was moving out, our furniture was moving in. That's just a little sidelight of some of the housing problems in wartime.

Peter Spectre: You were in Norfolk for a while.

Admiral O'Neill: Six months.

Peter Spectre: Well, your wife was there for quite a while. This is something that seldom comes out. What was life like in Norfolk for the families of men and officers who were off at sea?

Admiral O'Neill: Well, it was livable. There for a number of years there'd been feeling between the service people and the civilians in Norfolk; that's an open secret. There were no serious confrontations or anything like that, but there was a dividing line there. There was a gulf between the two. They got along all right during the war. A great many of the civilians there tried to be helpful, for example, in finding a place to live. I think one of the reasons for the feeling was the fact that when the ships would grant liberty down there, some of the crew would get a little bit boisterous on shore, and they would fill the streets. During the war, when several of the ships would send their liberty parties ashore, the street would be solid with white hats.

Peter Spectre: I was there once a few years ago, and about ten ships had come in from some operation. It was a Saturday afternoon, and they all granted leave at the same time; there was just a huge crowd.

Admiral O'Neill: That's it. It was even worse in wartime because of the amount of ships in there.

Peter Spectre: What were your duties as district commander, especially in contrast with the duties of a district commander in peacetime.

Admiral O'Neill: At that time we were still in the Navy, and my immediate boss was the Navy commander of the Fifth Naval District; I was on his staff. I was the senior Coast Guard officer, actually, on his staff, but he told me, "You just go ahead and carry on your duties, and we'll have a conference every once in a while." We had aids to navigation, beach patrol, port security—that was one of the big items—and ordinary assistance work, what little there was. One of the things the Navy found very helpful to them, particularly around the harbors, were the aids to navigation. If they wanted lights extinguished for blackout purposes, the Coast Guard could do that. Or they would want buoys moved, anchor marker buoys, and things like that. All they'd have to do was say, "Look, can you move this light from here to there?" and our buoy tenders would handle that for them.

Peter Spectre: Since the Coast Guard was part of the Navy, and the Navy had actual control over the Fifth Naval District, what is now the Fifth Coast Guard District, were there any Navy men who were assigned to what are normally considered Coast Guard duties?

Admiral O'Neill: None to my knowledge.

Peter Spectre: So you were still working as an autonomous force?

Admiral O'Neill: Oh, yes. We had no Navy people assigned as liaison officers or anything like that.

Peter Spectre: Did you feel that you were up to the job—qualified and able to handle the situation?

Admiral O'Neill: I had no misgivings about that. I had no feelings at all, no inferiority complexes. Then I forget when the Coast Guard was transferred back to the Treasury Department.

Peter Spectre: When did the war end in relation to your career?

Admiral O'Neill: It ended while I was district commander in August of '45. There was a big celebration in the streets of Norfolk. They didn't tear the place apart; it was a peaceful celebration.

Peter Spectre: You were still in Norfolk when all this happened?

Admiral O'Neill: Yes. Then I guess it was sometime in early January—Admiral Farley had succeeded Admiral Waesche as Commandant.[*]

Peter Spectre: When did Admiral Waesche die?[†]

Admiral O'Neill: I don't recall. I know he had cancer, and he was a very sick man there toward the end of his tour as Commandant. His voice was so bad that he had to have a

---

[*] Admiral Russell R. Waesche, USCG, served as Commandant of the Coast Guard from June 1936 to December 1945. Admiral Joseph F. Farley, USCG, served as Commandant of the Coast Guard from 1 January 1946 to 31 December 1949.
[†] Admiral Waesche died of cancer on 17 October 1946.

microphone placed on his desk in front of him, so when he had a conference he had to speak in the microphone, or they wouldn't have been able to hear him.

Peter Spectre: Did he die after he left office?

Admiral O'Neill: Yes.

Peter Spectre: And Admiral Farley was the Assistant Commandant?

Admiral O'Neill: No, he wasn't the Assistant Commandant. He was a rear admiral and then fleeted up to four stars, because at that time that was a four-star job. Right after the first of January, he arranged a meeting there in a friend's home, just a little private get-together. He asked me and Esther to come up; it was just a social affair. He and I and a couple of other officers were out in one room, and he asked me who I thought ought to be Assistant Commandant. I gave him the names of three officers, and he said, "What about you?"

I said, "I'm very happy in Norfolk." I'd just gotten my feet on the ground there. I'd been inspecting the units, the lifeboat stations, the radio stations, and port security units, and I was very happy; we had a nice house. Nothing more was said. Then shortly after that, maybe a week or two, he called me on the phone and said, "Your name has been sent over to the White House recommending you for appointment to Assistant Commandant."

Well, that was quite a surprise. All I could do was say, "Thank you very much." Then the appointment went through, and we moved up to Washington in February, as I recall. We rented an apartment from a friend for a while until we could find a place to live. Then my career as Assistant Commandant started right then and there.

Peter Spectre: You became rear admiral at the same time?

Admiral O'Neill: Yes.

Peter Spectre: What does an Assistant Commandant do?

Admiral O'Neill: Well, actually, he's a super chief of staff for the Commandant. We do have now a chief of staff, but in those days he was sort of the go-between for the various division officers, like operations, personnel, engineering, all those, finance and supply—between them and the Commandant. He kept the Commandant advised on anything that he thought a Commandant wouldn't know about or hear about. He handled a lot of routine work—a tremendous amount of routine work—for the Commandant, that the Commandant wouldn't be interested in, but someone had to handle it. Papers had to be signed, orders signed, and sometimes a few differences would come about that had to be ironed out without having to go to the top authority on it. As the name implies, he was, and still is, an assistant to the top man. And he's the top man when the Commandant's sick or on leave, or on an official trip. He immediately becomes the acting Commandant and signs correspondence as acting.

Peter Spectre: At that time did the Coast Guard have what is called now an administrative assistant to the Commandant?

Admiral O'Neill: Yes.

Peter Spectre: What were his duties in relation to your duties?

Admiral O'Neill: Paperwork mostly, back in those days. I don't know what it is now. And then the Commandant, back in those days, had an aide who was also a pilot. Admiral Farley's aide and pilot, the four years he was Commandant, is now to be the new Commandant of the Coast Guard.

Peter Spectre: Admiral Bender?[*]

---

[*] Admiral Chester R. Bender, USCG, served as Commandant of the Coast Guard from 1 June 1970 to 31 May 1974. His oral history is in the Naval Institute collection.

Admiral O'Neill: Yes. He was Farley's pilot and aide, and a very able officer.

Peter Spectre: What happened to the commodores of the Coast Guard?

Admiral O'Neill: At the end of the war that was done away with. At the same time that the Navy cancelled that type of rank, the Coast Guard did the same.

Peter Spectre: Were the people who were commodores temporary appointments?

Admiral O'Neill: Yes.

Peter Spectre: So that some of them would have gone back to captain and some would have gone forward to rear admiral.

Admiral O'Neill: It was a temporary rank. I'm sure it was done to stay in step with the Army.

Peter Spectre: What were some of the things that occupied your time right after the war as Assistant Commandant, particularly in the area of demobilization?

Admiral O'Neill: One of the major things was the tremendous number of men that had to be demobilized and given all sorts of advice on what to do when they left the service, about the GI Bill of Rights.* All that was done out in the field, of course. But the readjustment to bring the service back from a wartime strength of X thousand men to peacetime strength—ships had to be laid up, small boats laid up, men had to be transferred around. We had to do a lot of shuffling around to make do, to keep the service functioning the best we could until we got settled down again into a peacetime routine. That was one of the biggest problems.

---

* The GI Bill, officially the Servicemen's Readjustment Act of 1944, provided educational assistance and other benefits to all veterans honorably discharged with six or more months of active service after 16 September 1940.

Peter Spectre: How did you decide how many people were going to leave, where they were going to go, who was going to stay, how the ranks were going to be retained or lost—and that sort of thing?

Admiral O'Neill: I didn't have any part of that, because we were a separate office. They called it a demobilization office that handled all those details.

Peter Spectre: Congress must have had something to say about what the size of the Coast Guard was going to be now that the war was over.

Admiral O'Neill: They do. That's measured primarily by the amount of money they allow the service. The service makes up a budget and asks for X million dollars to carry out these duties. They need so much money and so many men to carry out their duties. Then Congress will go along with us in most cases. There were always cuts, because they figured we were asking for more than we really needed, figuring we would get a cut anyway. It's a game, you know, that they think we're playing with them.

Peter Spectre: Did you play that game?

Admiral O'Neill: To a very limited degree. If a service is given a series of jobs to do, like the Coast Guard, everyone wants to do the best job he can. He wants a maximum number of men and boats that he thinks are necessary to do a super-duper job, not necessarily the minimum number of boats. So he asks for the money to provide for the number of men and boats and all the expenses involved in it; then it has to be defended before Congress. If they disagree, there isn't much you can do about it.

The congressional appropriation bills go into the House first; then from there they go to the Senate. Sometimes, in appearing before the Senate, the Senate would restore some of the money that the House deleted. This idea of asking for twice as much as you think you need so that if they cut you 50% you can still carry on, that isn't true. But that idea came about because if you want do to the job properly, you figure you need so much to do it with, and members of Congress sometimes won't agree with you. That's where the cuts usually come. But I'll say that the cuts were never so severe that we were seriously handicapped. We were disappointed many times and felt that we could only do a 75% job instead of 100% and things like that.

Peter Spectre: In this whole process of asking for resources to keep the Coast Guard going and asking for money to retain some of the men that you had in the service at the end of the war, what was your relationship with the Treasury Department? Did your budget go to the Treasury Department first and then to Congress? Did the Treasury Department actually do something with that budget, or was it more or less an automatic thing?

Admiral O'Neill: The budget is made up in Coast Guard Headquarters and goes to the Treasury Department. Then hearings are held in the Treasury Department between the budget officer and whoever is defending it for the Coast Guard. The Secretary of the Treasury may delete, on the recommendation of the Treasury budget officer, or he may go along with it as it is. The budget is rewritten there and goes to the Bureau of the Budget, where hearings are held with the Coast Guard representative defending the budget and explaining to the bureau why we're asking for this. As a rule, the Treasury budget officer will attend that meeting almost as an observer, because he had hand in cutting it in the first place. Then after the Bureau of the Budget gets through with it, it's rewritten again and sent to the Hill to the appropriations committee.* They schedule hearings, usually in January, but the budget originally leaves headquarters in September to go to the Treasury. Then hearings are held in the House, and then it goes to the Senate. If they disagree, they have a conference, and then it's approved, and the money is appropriated.

Peter Spectre: Did the Treasury Department give the Coast Guard's budget serious consideration? I don't mean this in a light way or a disparaging way, but did the Treasury Department consider the Coast Guard as more or less an autonomous force?

---

* "The Hill" refers to Capitol Hill in Washington, D.C., that is, the U.S. Congress.

Did it or did it not give serious consideration to the Coast Guard's affairs in relation to other Treasury Department functions?

Admiral O'Neill: I think there may have been times when that feeling came about. I know that when the Eisenhower Administration took over, I was Commandant then in '52. One of the first things the Secretary of the Treasury did was direct the Coast Guard to furnish him with convincing information why the Coast Guard should stay in the Treasury Department.

Peter Spectre: Who was the Secretary?

Admiral O'Neill: George Humphrey. He would not accept the argument that just because it had always been in the Treasury Department, since its inception in 1790, as to why it should be there then. So the Assistant Commandant, Admiral Richmond, and I and several of the officers, had many conferences about it.* Several of our bright young officers were assigned solely to the job of preparing reasons as to why the Coast Guard belonged in the Treasury Department. One of them was that as a reserve of the Navy, we were better off in another department rather than in the Navy itself. Another very substantial argument was that we were a regulating agency and an enforcing agency, and that worked hand in hand to some extent, and there was no reason why the Coast Guard should be transferred to Commerce. That was what was behind all this—part would go into the Navy, and part would go to Commerce. That took about six months of work and finally died down.

As far as the budget was concerned, approving the budget, Secretary Humphrey wanted to make a cut, and he couldn't understand why the Coast Guard was carrying on this ocean station patrol, which cost $15 million. He wanted to know why and who we were doing that work for. Well, we were doing that work in cooperation with the Navy on this early warning system. We were out there to aid commercial planes flying the Atlantic and the Pacific. We were out there also in regard to having ships not too far

---

* Rear Admiral Alfred C. Richmond, USCG, served as Assistant Commandant of the Coast Guard, 1950-54. He was subsequently Commandant, 1954-62. His oral history is in the Naval Institute collection.

away from potential distress areas, where a ship would catch on fire or spring a leak and start to sink. That was regular search-and-rescue work. Anyway, he wanted to make a cut, so he said, "You do a lot of that work for the Navy; let the Navy pay for it." So he cut $15 million out of our budget, and the Navy picked up the check for it, because they wanted the Coast Guard to carry on these duties.

Peter Spectre: What did the Navy have to say about this in the meantime? Did he cut the $15 million before the Navy said they would pick up the tab, or was this worked out?

Admiral O'Neill: When he said he was going to cut the $15 million, we immediately went to the Navy and said, "How about this?" And they said they would pay for it. After my time I think the $15 million was put back in the Treasury, but the Navy was paying the bill the last two years that I was on duty there as Commandant.

Peter Spectre: Whose idea was it for Secretary Humphrey to ask the question, "Why is the Coast Guard in the Treasury Department?"? Was his intent to get rid of the Coast Guard in the Treasury Department, or to prove to somebody else that was asking the question, that the Coast Guard belonged in the Treasury Department?

Admiral O'Neill: That's hard to say. I think that idea came about from a study headed by Milton Eisenhower.* I'm not too sure of that, but I know there was a study made of all government departments in Washington—reorganization of everything. I think one of the recommendations in that was that the Coast Guard should be transferred mostly to Commerce. That would be the search and rescue; the lighthouses which had been in Commerce originally; marine inspection go back to Commerce.

The military part of the Coast Guard was to be transferred to the Navy and perhaps absorbed by the Navy, or function as a separate organization like the Marine Corps. I think that's where he got the idea, but where he stood personally I don't know. He was a very difficult man to talk to excerpt on a social occasion. All of our dealings—99% of our dealings with him while he was Secretary were with the Assistant Secretary,

---

* Dr. Milton Eisenhower was the brother of President Dwight Eisenhower.

Chapman Rose.[*] He'd been one of Humphrey's legal men and advisors in his enterprises on the lakes and elsewhere. We figured that if we could convince Mr. Rose that the Treasury was the logical place for the Coast Guard, we were quite certain that he would convince Humphrey, because Humphrey leaned heavily on Rose for information and advice.

Peter Spectre: Do you think that Rose was particularly qualified from his past for having more or less administrative control over the Coast Guard?

Admiral O'Neill: Yes, I think so. He was a very intelligent man and a man who was reasonable to work with. You could discuss things with him, pro and con. I always thought that he was a very good friend of the Coast Guard and an able administrator. I think he did a good job.

Peter Spectre: Did he work in other areas besides the Coast Guard?

Admiral O'Neill: I think Customs was also under him and maybe the Secret Service. There were two or three of those agencies in the Treasury Department under him.

Peter Spectre: Who was Secretary of the Treasury under Truman before the Eisenhower Administration?

Admiral O'Neill: John Snyder.[†]

Peter Spectre: How were your relations with him?

Admiral O'Neill: Great. Very pleasant and cordial. He and President Truman were good friends. He and I got talking one day about how no President had ever visited the Coast

---

[*] H. Chapman Rose served as Assistant Secretary of the Treasury, 1953-55, and as Under Secretary of the Treasury, 1955-56. Rose was a lawyer who previously in his career served as secretary to Supreme Court Associate Justice Oliver Wendell Holmes in 1931-32.
[†] John W. Snyder served as Secretary of the Treasury from 25 June 1946 to 20 January 1953.

Guard Academy, and he said, "You know, I think maybe we could get President Truman to go up there. I'll have a talk with him." And he did. So President Truman went up there on a visit, not to make a speech or anything. He went up on a special train car from Washington, and he visited the Academy and some of the classrooms. That was a big morale booster for the service; it added to our prestige to have the President for the first time visit the Academy.

Peter Spectre: The Coast Guard Academy had already moved to its present position?

Admiral O'Neill: Oh yes, that was the new Academy.

Peter Spectre: When did the Academy move?

Admiral O'Neill: I think it was about 1935-36 to its present location.

Peter Spectre: Did you have anything to do with the acquiring of the sailing ship, the *Eagle*?*

Admiral O'Neill: No, that was referred to Admiral Farley, and he handled that. I knew there was a discussion as to whether we should accept the *Eagle* and use her as a training ship. There were arguments for it and arguments against it. I guess he himself finally made the final argument.

Peter Spectre: Do you remember what the arguments were?

Admiral O'Neill: The arguments against were why train young boys these days on a sailing ship when there were no sailing ships except two or three training ships in a few of the foreign nations. Their argument was that it would be much better to train them on

---

* USCGC *Eagle* (WIX-327) is a 295-foot-long, 1,816-ton, three-masted bark used for sail training by the Coast Guard Academy. She was built in Hamburg, Germany, in the mid-1930s as the training ship *Horst Wessel* for the German Navy. She was transferred to the United States in January 1946 as part of German reparations in the aftermath of World War II and commissioned by the Coast Guard that year.

modern Coast Guard cutters. The argument for was that it brought back some of the old traditions of the sea, and it also gave the cadets a chance to acquire self-reliance. When they're up on the mast and all the yardarms, there's an old saying, "One hand for the ship and one hand for yourself."

Also, I think it added a great deal to the prestige of the Coast Guard as a public relations matter, too, because the *Eagle* has been, I think, a bonanza as far as public relations is concerned, the Academy especially. I think one of the most beautiful pictures was when President Kennedy was in office.[*] The *Eagle* came in from a cruise and moored down at the Navy Yard, and the cadets manned the yards. I was invited as a spectator, and I saw President Kennedy come down. When he saw the ship there with the sails furled and all the yards manned by cadets, he just stood there and looked. He just couldn't believe what he had seen. I know he was very much in favor of sailing.

Of course, the Coast Guard Academy uses various types of small sailing boats, but the sailing of the *Eagle* was entirely different. The pros finally won out, and I think it was a good thing that they did, because I think the *Eagle* has been a real asset in training young men.

Peter Spectre: What did the Treasury Department and Congress have to say, because the funds to operate it had to be approved?

Admiral O'Neill: I don't know the details on that, but there was never apparently any trouble getting the money to run the *Eagle*. Of course, the money to operate the *Eagle* would come out of the general fund, and no one in Congress that I ever heard about was opposed to it.

Peter Spectre: Where would it have gone if the Coast Guard hadn't taken it?

Admiral O'Neill: I don't know. Maybe the Navy would have found some use for it.

---

[*] John F. Kennedy served as President of the United States from 20 January 1961 until he was assassinated on 22 November 1963.

Peter Spectre: Do you know if the Naval Academy ever considered it?

Admiral O'Neill: I don't know if they did or not. The ship, as I understand, was taken over by the Navy in this reparations business, and I assume that they asked the Coast Guard if they could use it. The Coast Guard had used sailing ships in the not too far distant years. The *Alexander Hamilton* was both steam and sail, and she was a training ship. I think perhaps that may have been how the Navy happened to think of the Coast Guard and offered the *Eagle* to us.

Peter Spectre: How did it come about that you became Commandant?

Admiral O'Neill: At the time, of course, I was Assistant Commandant, and Admiral Farley recommended me. That's about all I can say. Maybe he thought I would make a good Commandant.

Peter Spectre: Were there any other officers considered that you know of?

Admiral O'Neill: Not that I know of. There may have been other officers considered, but Admiral Farley had to deal with Secretary Snyder on that. He had to recommend to Snyder, and if Snyder went along, then my name went to the White House. If the President approved, then to the Senate for confirmation. Theoretically, the Commandant is appointed by the President, but practically he's appointed by the Secretary of the department. And the Secretary of the department leans on the Commandant to recommend a successor. He doesn't have to go along with him. I imagine the odds were that other officers were considered, because I was only one of many, and I was junior to many officers, which actually isn't the best.

Peter Spectre: Did all this go on with you unaware of it while it was going on?

Admiral O'Neill: I knew that there was some delay there, and I assumed that it was probably due to whether they were weighing the merits and demerits of other officers that might be appointed in lieu of myself, but I had no definite information.

Peter Spectre: There was a delay in time?

Admiral O'Neill: Yes. My appointment wasn't approved right away. There was a hiatus there when Admiral Farley became a little bit upset about it, and I think he kind of faced up to the Secretary and asked him in simple language to do something right away, because it was hanging fire.

Peter Spectre: Had Farley retired?

Admiral O'Neill: No, he was still on active duty.

Peter Spectre: Do you have any idea why the delay occurred, or was this something that was beyond you?

Admiral O'Neill: There was some information that some officer, or small group of officers, questioned whether I should be Commandant or not, because of the fact that they thought I was opposed to aviation—that I was unfriendly toward that branch of operations, which was ridiculous. But there was some indication that there was a holdup for that reason. The Secretary of the Treasury had heard, someone had advised him—ill advisedly—that if I was appointed Commandant, aviation would suffer. But it blew over, and nothing very terrible ever happened to aviation.

Peter Spectre: Admiral, what was your feeling toward aviation before you were Commandant and when you were Commandant?

Admiral O'Neill: Well, aviation was an arm of operations. We used the planes for search and rescue. It was like the Lighthouse Service. That was an arm of operations. Our oceangoing ships and our small inshore patrol boats—all those were arms of operations, the same as aviation. It was all under one heading.

Peter Spectre: What did the aviators feel? Did they feel that they were a separate entity? Is that where the conflict was?

Admiral O'Neill: Yes, mostly. They felt like they were a separate service, but that no longer prevailed.

Peter Spectre: But it did at one time?

Admiral O'Neill: Yes, but it was never serious. The aviators were referred to as flyboys and things like that. There was a little feeling and some feeling also because the aviators were on flight pay, and a great many of them, contemporaries and classmates of officers, were getting more money. That always enters the picture to some extent. But it was never serious. It was just talk and bantering sometimes. A lot of it was jokingly said.

Peter Spectre: How did the aviators want to be treated?

Admiral O'Neill: There was a feeling among some of them for a separate office in headquarters—I mean an aviation department. Take them out of operations and put them separately. Most of us never agreed to that and haven't agreed to it today, as far as I know. In regard to my feeling toward aviation, my son-in-law, Richard Penn, is an aviator. He was on a cutter when he and Patricia were married. He took his training at Pensacola and became a flier. He was in aviation up until he retired last year.[*]

When I went in as Commandant, I picked an aviator for an aide. It was recommended to me that I pick a line officer as an aide and then have an aviator assigned to fly me when I made trips by plane. But I didn't go along with that idea, because Admiral Farley's aide was an aviator, now-Admiral Bender; he was then a lieutenant

---

[*] Commander Richard T. Penn, Jr., USCG, Coast Guard Academy class of 1949, retired from active duty on 1 August 1969.

commander. It worked out beautifully with Farley to have an aviator as an aide, and I followed along the same idea. The way I picked my aide, I called in various officers to ask them to recommend an aviator as an aide, and I got several names from aviators. I called several of them in and talked to them about I was looking for an aide. I picked the one who was mostly recommended by the aviators; they said he was an aviators' aviator. William A. Jenkins was my aide for four years.[*]

Peter Spectre: What about the Assistant Commandant when you became Commandant?

Admiral O'Neill: I recommended Admiral Richmond as Assistant Commandant and sent his name over to the Secretary.

Peter Spectre: Was this the normal course of events, that after the new Commandant was appointed that he make the recommendation for Assistant Commandant?

Admiral O'Neill: That's right. And then the same thing came up. There was a long delay because a small group—I think maybe one or two—of the aviators brought up the same thing, that Richmond was opposed to aviation, which was absolutely nonsense. But there was a hiatus there again, and finally I convinced Snyder that Richmond was the logical man. He had actually been serving as chief of staff, fairly familiar with all the details, the operations of the Coast Guard, familiar with headquarters organization. So after a delay again, he was appointed.

Peter Spectre: Was he what was then the deputy chief of staff before he became Assistant Commandant?

Admiral O'Neill: He was the chief of staff. I don't know what the title is.

---

[*] Lieutenant Commander William A. Jenkins, USCG, eventually became a rear admiral and served as superintendent of the Coast Guard Academy.

Peter Spectre: I think the title runs deputy chief of staff.*

What about your personal feeling about Admiral Richmond? Was he a friend of ours? Had you know him for a long time?

Admiral O'Neill: Yes, I had known him since we were first instructors at the old Coast Guard Academy at Fort Trumbull. We were both in instructions staff. Then we were shipmates on one of the destroyers for a while. I knew him very well. We were good service friends. I felt he was the best man for the job. He later on became Commandant.

Peter Spectre: How did the Lighthouse Service fit in with the rest of the service?

Admiral O'Neill: Very well. When the Lighthouse Service was taken over by the Coast Guard, the senior officers in the Lighthouse Service were commissioned various ranks.† Some of them were appointed rear admiral, some commodore. They were very able men; they were mostly all college men.

Peter Spectre: They had been civilians before then?

Admiral O'Neill: Yes. They fitted in very well, and that transition went along very smoothly.

Peter Spectre: How much in size, in proportion to the rest of the service, did they add to it?

Admiral O'Neill: Oh, I would say maybe 25%. As far as equipment is concerned, I think that would be about the percentage. If you consider the buoys, nun buoys and spar buoys, and these little fixed lights on the rivers, and all, I think at one time there were

---

* In the late 1940s Richmond was an assistant chief of staff for planning and control. He became Assistant Commandant in March 1950. On 1 May 1951, when the Coast Guard reorganized, he was designated Chief of Staff and continued to serve as Assistant Commandant.
† On 7 July 1939 the Bureau of Lighthouses in the Department of Commerce ceased to exist. It functions were transferred to the Coast Guard as of that date.

something like 30,000 aids to navigation included in all these little things. That would raise the percentage much higher than 25%.

Peter Spectre: Now they're up to 50,000.

What about your relations with the Navy when you were Assistant Commandant and Commandant?

Admiral O'Neill: Very cordial, very pleasant.

Peter Spectre: Did you maintain constant liaison with them?

Admiral O'Neill: Yes. We also appointed a Coast Guard officer to the Navy Department as liaison, where he could handle a lot of the details.

Peter Spectre: What types of things did that involve with the Navy? You mentioned that the ocean station program was handled with the Navy. What other types of things?

Admiral O'Neill: A great deal of it you might call routine. I think the most important thing at the time was the ocean station program.

Peter Spectre: What type of planning did you do, like modernizing the ships, building new ships, what the Coast Guard was going to continue to do, what the Coast Guard would de-emphasize in future years?

Admiral O'Neill: That was developed right after I retired, but the planning ahead during my tour was done usually in conference with the heads of our offices and departments in headquarters, like engineer and operations, the chief of staff, the Assistant Commandant. It was largely planning ahead to replace obsolete planes, asking for money, replace obsolete ships, building new ships, building additional patrol boats, aids to navigation.

We had a research and development department. They would come up with very sensible recommendations for new types of aids and ships. Then aviation would come up with their figures on what planes should be cast aside and new planes added, new types of planes. Then that would mean conferences between our aviation section and naval aviation and the Air Force. We bought planes from the Air Force on contract. The Air Force would have a contract with some airplane manufacturing company, and we would ask to buy three or four of those planes as they came off the assembly line on Navy or Air Force contracts.

Interview Number 4 with Admiral Merlin O'Neill, U.S. Coast Guard (Retired)
Place: Admiral O'Neill's home in Lusby, Maryland
Date: Sunday, 7 March 1971
Interviewer: Peter Spectre

Peter Spectre: Admiral, the last time that we talked, which was quite a while ago, we covered some of the points that took place when you were Assistant Commandant and Commandant of the Coast Guard. I wonder if you could talk some more about that period, particularly right now about what happened to the Coast Guard Reserve after the Second World War. Would you fill me in a little bit on that?

Admiral O'Neill: Of course, at the end of World War II we were faced with what I would call a serious cutback in personnel, our enlisted personnel and our reserve officer corps. We set up demobilization centers in various parts of the country. At the same time with our cutback in our forces that had been built up during World War II, we were faced with the problem of carrying on our regular peacetime duties and at the same time reducing our forces. I don't recall the exact number, but during World War II we had an enrollment of all hands of probably close to 100,000 personnel of all categories.

The reserve officer corps, as I call it, was seriously cut back and reduced to just a handful of reserve officers. Then a few years later we began to build it up very, very slowly.

We had no, you might say, training ships back in those days as established later on to take reservists out on two weeks' training cruises, and schools for them, and the famous drill periods that they were required to take. It was a time when the service was almost demoralized there for a while, while we were making a shift from wartime duties to peacetime duties, and with the intended cutback of appropriations, as it always happens in cases of that kind.

Peter Spectre: Were the reserves funded separately from the regular Coast Guard?

Admiral O'Neill: No. I would say "no" to this extent: we would ask for appropriations, a certain amount, for reserve personnel. That is, expense for carrying on the reserves. But a great deal of the funds came not only from those appropriations but from the appropriations for the regular Coast Guard.

It was a very trying time. A great many of the reservists, I'm sure, were anxious to remain in the Coast Guard as part of the permanent establishment, but we just couldn't keep them. We didn't have the money of our own regular appropriations, and there was very little money appropriated by Congress for carrying on. They all said, "The war is over. You don't need a reserve. You don't need port security. You don't need reservists to supplement your own personnel aboard your ships and aboard your stations." And that's why there was a pinch in funds.

I know it was almost heartbreaking at times to let so many able reserve officers go when they wanted to stay in the service. They were good, competent men, in all categories.

Peter Spectre: What about the women's reserve?

Admiral O'Neill: This was in the same category. The SPARS organization was cut from thousands—I don't know the exact number—just to a handful, maybe a dozen or two commissioned ones and a few enlisted SPARS.* That built up a little bit more later on, but the SPARS organization is still very, very small.

Peter Spectre: During this period of time after the war, we did talk in our last interview about the demobilization of the regular Coast Guard.

As you faced the problem, what did you yourself envision the Coast Guard being after the war was over? I'm sure that there were plenty of other people that had their own opinion as well, for instance, the Secretary of the Treasury or the President or the Congress. What did you as the Assistant Commandant and then the Commandant see the

---

* SPAR, meaning a Coast Guard woman, is a term originated in World War II by Captain Dorothy Stratton, USCGR, the first director of the SPARs. It is a contraction of the Coast Guard's motto and its meaning, "Semper Paratus, Always Ready." Stratton's oral history is in the Naval Institute collection.

role of the Coast Guard as being after the Second World War and before the Korean War?

Admiral O'Neill: In other words, we would go back to what I call the old-time peacetime duties. It involved search and rescue. That was primarily our function at that time, and that would include our lifeboat stations.

During World War II the Lighthouse Service was merged with the Coast Guard, and also merchant marine inspection became a permanent part of the Coast Guard. So then we thought we'd have our full-time duties, plus these additional duties that were transferred to us in the way of aids to navigation and merchant marine inspection. That's what we were looking toward at the end of the war—as having a Coast Guard with the old-time regular duties, plus these additional duties that we acquired during World War II.

Peter Spectre: What about the merchant marine inspection part? Did you welcome this particular function to the Coast Guard?

Admiral O'Neill: Yes. Personally I thought it was an excellent thing that we should take over the merchant marine inspection, also the aids to navigation. I thought those fell right directly in line with Coast Guard activities and duties.

Peter Spectre: What about acquiring those two—one being the Lighthouse Service and the other being part of the Commerce Department, the Bureau of Marine Inspection?

On one hand you're bringing new people into the service, both from the Lighthouse Service and the Bureau of Marine Inspection, yet you're also trying to kick out old people because it's the end of the war. How did this fit into the scheme of things? Where does your loyalty lie, and other people's loyalties lie, when you're going to say this guy has to go or this guy has to go?

In the meantime, some other people have come in because they have to come in. There must be a lot of friction and emotions about that.

Admiral O'Neill: I think there's no doubt there was some feelings there and some mixed emotions. What actually happened, the merchant marine inspection, as we called it, had become militarized, and the same for the Lighthouse Service.

In order to take those two services over and bring them into the Coast Guard, it was necessary to keep regular men that they had had employed for years—they were experienced men—in order to operate these two new services that we took over. The overall command was vested in the Commandant. He had as his assistants former officers of Merchant Marine Inspection and the Lighthouse Service commissioned. They became commissioned regular Coast Guard officers.

A great many of the others, the lesser ranks and ratings, continued to be in the civilian status. Some were commissioned, and some were appointed as boatswains, and some were enlisted, but the great majority of them maintained their civilian status. Then, as they retired, regular Coast Guard men took their places.

The chief of the Bureau of Marine Inspection and Navigation became the chief of Merchant Marine Inspection in the Coast Guard.* He was appointed a rear admiral. When he retired, others who had had experience in Merchant Marine Inspection took over his position, and eventually regular Coast Guard officers became chief of the Bureau of Marine Inspection and Navigation—the Merchant Marine Inspection, as we call it.

Peter Spectre: How did you plan on the filling of the lower echelons, as the more senior members of the Merchant Marine Inspection retired and used up the body of people that they brought into the service with them? How did the Coast Guard and you, as one of the planners of the Coast Guard at that time, plan on filling these ranks of people in Merchant Marine Inspection? Were you gong to rely on the Coast Guard Academy or other schools or special training programs?

Admiral O'Neill: Both. We relied partly on graduates of the Coast Guard Academy, and also we took in personnel from the merchant marine. We commissioned them in the Coast Guard, men who had many years' experience aboard ships in various capacities,

---

* On 28 February 1942 the Commerce Department's Bureau of Navigation and Steamboat Inspection was transferred to the Treasury Department and became a function of the Coast Guard.

mates and engineers. As far as I know, we're still doing that. We took in a certain number—I don't recall the exact number, but there were a great many who came in from civilian life who had spent a good part of their lives handling services.

Peter Spectre: The thing that I still don't understand, maybe the problem didn't exist, on one hand people were being forced to leave the service after the war. The war was over, and the Coast Guard needed no people, and these people were Coast Guardsmen. On the other hand, there were two new services that had come into the Coast Guard during the war who were going to take the place really of Coast Guardsmen. How did you reconcile the two, or were there no problems?

Admiral O'Neill: There was no problem there, because these new people, let's call them, that were brought in from those two services that we're talking about—they didn't take jobs over from regular Coast Guardsmen and force the Coast Guardsmen out. These were two entirely new and different functions.

We brought one group of experienced men in under the wing of the Coast Guard to operate the aids to navigation, the Lighthouse Service, and the same with the Merchant Marine Inspection. Their various inspectors in the old Bureau of Marine Inspection and Navigation came along with the administrative crew. There wasn't a great number of them in either case. They were both small services.

For example, the Merchant Marine Inspection had boiler inspectors and hull inspectors and men of that kind; they didn't displace any regular Coast Guardsmen. These Coast Guard Reservists that we had during World War II—their duties were entirely different. A great many of them were assigned to the amphibious forces and duties of that kind. When the amphibious force was disbanded—that included the Coast Guard part—those were the reserve officers who were let go because we had no place for them. I use that as an example. And so they were released. It was in that group, to my personal knowledge, that so many of them were anxious to stay in the Coast Guard permanently. But, sad as it was to us, we just couldn't hold onto them.

There were other cases of reserve officers who were instructors in some of our schools. For example, our school in New London, not the Academy, some refer to it as our training school in Groton, Connecticut. We had some reserve officers that were assigned there as instructors. They'd been teachers in high schools, for example, in civilian life. They were not in the amphibious force. They'd always been teachers, they were teachers, and they wanted to keep on teaching in our schools, but we couldn't keep them. That's another case where it was difficult to let them go, on account of the cutback and the lack of funds.

Peter Spectre: The next thing I'd like to get into is the actual physical condition of the Coast Guard during this period. You were assistant head of the Coast Guard during the time when the ships that the service had were starting to get old. During the war a lot of the Coast Guard cutters were really Navy ships, manned by Coast Guardsmen, which I understand went back to the Navy at the end of the war. In the meantime, the Coast Guard cutters that were built during the '30s had been through a world war and were starting to get old. What were your plans for rebuilding—not only ships but everything else, boats, buildings, and the rest of the physical part?

Admiral O'Neill: That's a good expression, the physical part of it.

There were shore stations and small boats and seagoing cutters. It was always a question when the budget was made up to ask for a certain number of ships and a rebuilding program. Congress gave us some money, never as much as we asked for, to replace the ships that were old and obsolete and had served their usefulness. That's been going on for a great many years, of replenishing not only our ships and shore stations but our planes. Our planes were old, and they had to be replaced.

As I say, Congress gave us enough money to keep going and replenish the stations and the ships that were most in need of replacing, but it was a struggle, and sometimes a disappointment, not to get the ships that we wanted.

Peter Spectre: Can you think of any examples of things that you particularly wanted to have during that period of time that were cut from the budget, and the reasons why they were cut, and who cut them? Was it at the Treasury Department level or the Bureau of the Budget level or Congress itself?

Admiral O'Neill: I don't recall any specific cases like that; it was all in one lump sum. For example, if we wanted money to build six new seagoing cutters, we might get money from Congress to build two. I just use those figures as an example, but that's what I mean by the cutback.

We used to try to convince the Budget and Congress, of course, the Appropriations Committee, the fact that some of our planes that were still flying in our search-and-rescue work were so obsolete that they were not deemed safe. Although I don't recall any serious accidents where we had any great loss, it was a risk to some extent of men flying planes that were old. It was always a struggle to keep them up and make them reasonably safe for flying; the same was true of the cutters.

There's no one specific case that I can recall right now.

Peter Spectre: I came across an interesting fact that I'm sure you know, but I never had known. It was one of those things you just happen to be reading something and discover it. The Coast Guard acquired from the Navy on loan during the early '50s quite a few destroyer escorts. I'm not sure what they were used for. Do you remember anything about that?

Admiral O'Neill: Yes. We took over a number; I don't recall the exact number. Some of them were known as seaplane tenders. They were not large ships; they were in the 325-foot category. They were used primarily in the ocean stations. We set up stations in the Atlantic and the Pacific, what we call ocean stations. They were there to report on weather and to act as rescue ships in case of a transatlantic plane going down. There were a number of cases where they rescued entire crews of planes, both in the Atlantic and the Pacific.

Peter Spectre: I knew about the seaplane tenders, which we still have some of now, the AVPs. The *Absecon* is one of them; the *Unimak* is another. But these were destroyer escorts.

Admiral O'Neill: They were a small version of a destroyer, and at a distance looked like destroyers.

Peter Spectre: Some of those same destroyer escorts when in the Navy were used for a seaward extension of the DEW Line, just an early warning system.* Do you remember anything about those?

Admiral O'Neill: Very little. There weren't very many of the destroyer escorts that we took over from the Navy. There were only a few, but they were used for ocean stations. The best ships that we got from the Navy were the AVPs.

Peter Spectre: How did you arrange for the transfer of various ships from the Navy? Did the Navy give you a list and say, "These are the ships that we are going to decommission, and if you're interested come and look at them"? Or did you go to the Navy and say, "We need a lot of ships. Do you have any you can spare?"

Admiral O'Neill: It was a case that we were in the market for ships, and we knew that the Navy was decommissioning a number of those ships that were comparable to our seagoing cutters. It was just a question of contacting the Navy and arranging for them to be transferred to the Coast Guard. It's a very simple procedure, just a little paper work.

Where they, for example, had no crew aboard on a number of these ships, we would send a crew aboard and take them over. In most cases they were in good condition. They weren't run down; they had been active and hadn't been laid up for years like in the old back channel Philadelphia days, where it would take a year to recondition them and repair them. These were ships that were practically ready to go. They weren't brand-new ships, of course, but a great many of them were newer than ours.

Peter Spectre: Did this cost you money?

---

* DEW Line—Distant Early Warning Line, a chain of radar sites built 1,200 miles from the North Pole in the early 1950s as a means of detecting Soviet bombers approaching the United States over the Arctic.

Admiral O'Neill: I don't recall any money in the transaction being involved there. The only money transaction that I recall was when the money—I think it was approximately $15 million—was cut out of our budget by the Treasury Department for the operation of the ocean stations. Then the Navy picked up the tab on those, because the Navy was interested in this ocean station program.

These ships were not only useful to the country and the Navy for weather reporting and rescue of planes, but as part of the early warning system for the Navy. I do remember that $15 million that the Navy picked up and carried on for us.

Peter Spectre: I'd like to talk to you a little bit about when you were Commandant and Assistant Commandant. How were decisions made? Say you were Commandant, and you had a particular problem where a question came up, and the answer had to be provided. How were decisions made? Did you have a policy board that you consulted with? Did you rely on advisers and then make a decision? And then where did the Secretary of the Treasury come into all of this when the decision was made?

Admiral O'Neill: If it was a service problem, the Commandant has a staff. He has an Assistant Commandant, a chief of staff, and he has various heads of departments. Usually that big a problem would be studied under the direction of the chief of staff and the Assistant Commandant, and they would come out with the pros and cons of the problem. Then there'd be a meeting in the Commandant's office where all this would be thrashed out and the pros and cons gone over then. Then the decision made right then: "Let's do this and that, and don't do this and don't do that."

If it were a problem—I don't recall any right now—where the Treasury Department should get in on it, it would be taken up with the Secretary of the Treasury through the Assistant. There's an Assistant Secretary of the Treasury who had the immediate department control over the Coast Guard.

Sometimes in these problems he would make the decision on it after consulting with the Secretary of the Treasury. Very seldom would there be a meeting in the Secretary of the Treasury's office. He would talk it over, after consulting with the

Assistant Secretary, and the Assistant Secretary with the Commandant and the Assistant Commandant, and then the decision would be made.

For normal routine problems that had to be solved in the service, sometimes the Commandant would make the decision immediately without consulting—it was so obvious what the answer was, no need to study a problem if it was a simple one.

If it was complicated, it would be different, like when we were faced with the problem of trying to convince the Secretary that the Coast Guard shouldn't be broken up and part transferred to the Navy and part back to the Secretary of Commerce. That was a sizable problem and a terrific headache and a nightmare for a few months. And that required a great deal of staff study to bring up information and facts and arguments as to why the Coast Guard should stay in the Treasury Department. That went on for months. Several officers there at headquarters were on full-time duty working up all these various facts and figures and all to present to the Assistant Secretary and he, in turn, to the Secretary.

Peter Spectre: Who were some of the people, names, and personalities that you relied on most to help you in decisions that you had to make?

Admiral O'Neill: Mostly the Assistant Commandant, who was Admiral Richmond, and he in turn had as his right-hand man Stevens and Capron and the chief engineer, the heads of the departments at headquarters. He had all those to make these studies for him and with him. He and I would confer, sometimes just the two of us. We had a board meeting, department meeting, sometimes every day, sometimes once a week. Most of the spadework, as we called it, was done by the chief of planning control, chief of staff, and officers in those categories.

Peter Spectre: Who constituted the board? When your board met, all those people met?

Admiral O'Neill: It was the whole board, the heads of departments.

Peter Spectre: Who were some of the strong people in that, other than yourself?

Admiral O'Neill: I wasn't deeply strong; I was just sitting there on the throne.

The Assistant Commandant probably was the strongest member of the team, but he had some exceptionally able men at his beck and call. In other words, if it involved finance and supply, he could lean on him. A problem would come up, and he would call the chief of finance and supply to his office, and they'd go over the problem. It was up to the chief of finance and supply to present the case to Admiral Richmond. He would have to make his decision, and if it was a major one we would have a meeting on it and study the pros and cons—in other words, work staff studies.

Peter Spectre: This is a question that's always intrigued me—a lot of the people that I've worked for, I felt as if they were basing their decisions on one-sided information. Say, I worked for you, and somebody else works for you. You ask me a question, and I give you an answer that is coated quite a bit to my beliefs. Then you ask the same question to another fellow that works for you, and he gives you an answer coated by his beliefs. So you might get two separate thoughts on the same question.

What did you do yourself to make sure that you had been given objective facts? How did you check on the truth of what you were hearing?

Admiral O'Neill: Of course, you had to have confidence in the men that you were consulting. If you didn't have confidence in them, then you'd find somebody else. You had to realize that the top man, say, the Commandant, for example, would have a different opinion many times because he could see the overall picture. Whereas you, the other man who's telling me about this, in a way couldn't see the forest for the trees.

They had their own ideas, and they didn't look at it from the overall point of view—how it would go with the Appropriations Committee, could it be sold to the Appropriations Committee, or to the Secretary of the Treasury if he had the final say-so? You had to sift those things.

Sometimes you believed what the chief of one office would say, knowing that he was a little bit partial, and he figured that his job was probably the most important job in headquarters. And that's good. In other words, he feels that without finance and supply, headquarters would fold up. He sees all these immediate problems, and he looks at them, and he wants them done thus and so; that's the way he wants it. But that wouldn't necessarily be best for the overall Coast Guard. That's where somebody has to say, "That's all well and good, appreciate what you say, but it's got to be this way."

Sometimes the heads of offices were disappointed because their particular argument wasn't accepted in toto, but for the most part they would say, "Yes, you want it done this way, then that's the way it will be. You asked my opinion, and I said, 'Let's do it this way.' You say, 'No,' you want it done your way, then that's the way it will be."

Peter Spectre: Another interesting question is—if you were Commandant now, and I was the rank that I presently hold in the Coast Guard Reserve, lieutenant (junior grade), you would scare me to death, because the Commandant of the Coast Guard is an important person. If you left headquarters and went to a Coast Guard station, and you confronted a lieutenant (junior grade) the same as myself and asked a question, it would seem to me it would be very hard for you to get an honest answer. The lieutenant (junior grade) might give you an answer that he thought you would like to hear. This is a problem not only in the service; it happens anywhere else in the hierarchy of an organization. What did you do to cut through this type of thing? I'm sure you're aware that it existed. How would you get around that?

Admiral O'Neill: A lot depends on how the senior officer approaches the junior officer—in other words, a rear admiral approaching a lieutenant (junior grade) at a station or on board ship or whatever it may be. Let's use a station as an example. A friendly approach, where you immediately try to convince the junior that after all the admiral is a human being. You put the junior at ease first of all just by innocuous, harmless questions. Ask him if he's married, if he has a family, what activities he's been involved in in the last few days, what he's been doing. Put him at ease; it's the way you approach him.

If you start out with a rough and gruff attitude, naturally you create a case where you say he'd answer your questions the way he thought you'd want them answered. If you put him at ease, he would almost invariably give you an honest answer as to how he felt about it. I think that is always the best and only approach, if you wanted some information from him. You can apply that to enlisted men, too, and petty officers and chief petty officers. That's where you get a lot of information, from your noncommissioned officers. Put them at ease and then ask them a question, "How's the chow?" (You'd eventually find out how the food was aboard a ship.)

He'd invariably come out with an honest answer. He'd say, "It's excellent," or "It's terrible," or "There's room for lots of improvement."

I found that was my experience.

Peter Spectre: Did you ever feel that you weren't getting a straight story, especially when you were Commandant? You had a problem you were trying to solve, you asked for a staff study, or you just asked for the opinion of the people on your board. Did you ever reach a point on any subject where you thought you weren't getting a straight answer?

Admiral O'Neill: No, I don't recall anything like that. I knew that I was getting what you might call a partial answer, an answer that he thought was best for his own department. But not to mislead the Commandant or mislead him in any way or give him a dishonest answer—I never met up with an occasion like that in my time as Commandant.

Peter Spectre: In the last interview that we had we talked about when you became Commandant that there was a little bit of a problem at the beginning before you were actually confirmed over the aviation question. The aviation officers said that you weren't really for them, that you were really against them. If that's true, and you did become Commandant, you had to deal with the people in aviation then. Especially you had to deal with the people who opposed you before you became Commandant. What happened then? Was aviation under operations at that time?

Admiral O'Neill: Yes, aviation was an arm of operations.

The ones who opposed the appointment of the Commandant and the Assistant Commandant were just a handful. I would say there were only probably three or four that tried to stir up some trouble, but we didn't deal with them. We had officers in aviation there at headquarters, loyal men. We had no dealings at all with the dissidents. We took no action against them. Of course, we weren't certain who they were. We had rumors who two or three of them were, but we had no proof of it, and we didn't conduct any intelligence work to find out about it. We just glossed it over, forgot about it, and went ahead with our business.

Peter Spectre: Do you have any idea how they went about this? Did they call up the Secretary of the Treasury or—?

Admiral O'Neill: I don't know what the route was to him, but they got word to the Assistant Secretary or the Under Secretary, and he in turn maybe to the Secretary. But we don't know exactly how this was done unless it was through some friend of theirs, I think probably in some civilian capacity, who could carry the ball to the Secretary. In my opinion they never convinced the Secretary or the Under Secretary that the potential Commandant and Assistant Commandant were anti-aviation, because we weren't.

It was such a silly approach. Apparently the dissidents got the idea that the Coast Guard would never have any high-ranking officers in aviation because we were trying to belittle aviation and make it a very minor part of operations. I think some of the junior officers—and they weren't the belligerent type—had the feeling that there should be a separate office of aviation with a flag officer in command. That was the feeling among some, but it wasn't pursued very much. They talked about it. They said, "Why can't we have a flag officer here in aviation?"

Our aviation arm was small, and it had to be a part of operations, because it always has been and always will be a part of operations—search and rescue. Look at the work that aviation has done in the past and is doing today, especially with this new idea of using helicopters to take sick people off ships at sea if it's too rough to lower a small boat and row over there to pick them up from the side of a ship. It's got to be a part of operations.

Peter Spectre: Do you think that what happened then had any bearing on the selection of future Commandants? It brings to mind Admiral Smith, the just past Commandant, and the new one now, Admiral Bender—both aviators.

Do you think that the problems that occurred with you and Admiral Richmond may have made people aware of the fact that aviators might not be going as far as they should go? Do you have any thoughts on that?

Admiral O'Neill: Smith and Bender were both outstanding aviators. Knowing that we could not appoint a flag officer to head up aviation, we had to appoint an aviator—fleet him up to rear admiral rank. After they'd served a number of years in aviation, as you see, they turned in their wings, and they became just regular line officers. Some were passed over by selection boards, because they were still on active duty as aviators, and they couldn't select them because there was no billet for them in aviation. The minute they turned in their wings, they were promoted. There were several cases of that.

One was a very close personal friend of mine and still is, Admiral Olsen; he retired. He was head of aviation, and he was passed over. He was a captain then, a very excellent, able man. He was passed over, and it hurt him deeply, until he was convinced that if he would turn in his wings, there were billets for him then, because he'd been a line officer before he went into aviation. He was perfectly competent to take over a district. He was promoted to rear admiral and assigned as district commander, and he retired as a district commander. I cite his name as an example.[*]

Peter Spectre: That brings up a whole new area—your relationships with the district commanders.

The Coast Guard is a little bit unusual for a federal agency, and practically any agency, and that is that parts of the service are fairly autonomous. Not only is the service autonomous, Coast Guard districts do stand alone practically, depending, of course, who might be the district commander at that particular time. How were things when you were

---

[*] Rear Admiral Carl B. Olsen, USCG (Ret.). For another perspective on Admiral Olsen's case, see the Naval Institute oral history of Admiral Owen W. Siler, USCG (Ret.).

Commandant—the relationship between you and the district commanders? And you as representing the centralized Coast Guard as against the decentralized Coast Guard?

Admiral O'Neill: To begin with, when I was appointed Commandant, most of the district commanders had always been senior to me, and I was a little bit apprehensive at first as to how well they would function on a team. But I discovered pleasantly that there was no problem there at all; they were very loyal. They ran their own districts.

Every year we had a district commanders' conference. At that conference the first day all the district commanders came in with some of the heads of our departments there at headquarters. We had an overall meeting in the Commandant's office. (I don't know whether they do that today or not, but I think they do.) We'd just go over the basic plan, the overall plan of the conference, which usually lasted about three to four days.

Then, after that meeting would disband, we'd all go out to lunch somewhere, and then meet in the afternoon. They would then all meet with the chief of the office of engineering, and they would go over their problems with him. Then maybe the following morning they would meet with the chief of the office of operations and go over their problems with him. And in turn the chiefs of these different offices would advise the district commanders what headquarters problems were—whether it was money or building of ships or stationing of cutters.

For example, in operations the district commanders would say, "Look, we want the homeport of this ship transferred from this place to that place."

Then the chief of operations would say, "Now, just a minute. We have a political problem involved here. If we take that ship away from there, then one of the members of Congress is going to come storming down here on our heads. We've got to have a good argument before we make that change, in order to convince Congress that that is the best thing for the district."

To go back to dealing with the district commanders, I said they ran their own districts. If they had an immediate problem, they would send a radio to headquarters or call me on the telephone. If I wasn't there, they'd talk to the Assistant Commandant.

They'd say, "Look, we've got to have a decision on this right away." Then you'd have to give them a decision, because you can't wait to have another study or something like that.

Then, at the end of the conference, back in those days—this was started by my predecessor—probably the last afternoon all the district commanders would meet with the Commandant, none of the heads of departments. Sometimes the Commandant would call in the Assistant Commandant but nobody else. Then they could comment on what they were told by the heads of the departments at headquarters. They might say, "We don't agree with it. We told him what our problem was, and he didn't go along with it. Now we'd like for you to give this a little further study."

In that way, that would go over the head of the department, but that didn't happen very often, because the district commanders, a great many of them, had had duty in headquarters. They knew what headquarters' problems were, and we had a pretty good idea what their problems were. So we had to resolve the two and come up with a final answer to the best of all concerned. It worked out very well, and it's still working well.

Peter Spectre: Did you ever wish that they weren't as autonomous as they really are?

Admiral O'Neill: No, I think they should be. They should be allowed to be captain of their own ship. They're in the district, and they're right on top of things. Headquarters and the Commandant shouldn't step into the picture. Otherwise, they can't run the district, and the district commander has got to run his own district. And if he can't run it, you get somebody who can. I think it was a good arrangement, and it worked very well.

Peter Spectre: How aware were you of district problems, in view of the fact that you were probably one of the few Commandants of the Coast Guard who wasn't a district commander by himself? You were district commander of the Fifth District, but the Navy was really in command at that time that you were there. You were sort of like a chief of staff?

Admiral O'Neill: At first yes, and then just toward the end of my tour of duty there I became a full-fledged district commander under the Commandant of the Coast Guard. The Navy was out of it. That was just a couple of months.

Peter Spectre: Do you think from the experience that you had a good enough understanding of what the district—?

Admiral O'Neill: It would have been better if I had had more, a longer tour of duty as a district commander. I was there for six months, under the Navy for three or four months.

The Navy—he never said anything to me. He said, "If you have any problems, come down, and we'll talk them over." I never had any problem to bring up to him. I used to call on him occasionally, just to say, "Good morning," but he let me run the Coast Guard just the same as ever. He never interfered one way at all.

But it would have been better. If a man has had a year or two of district command experience, it's better for him when he goes in as Commandant, no doubt about it.

Peter Spectre: Naturally, you want people working closely for you, with you, people that you trust and that you know and that you understand, not only as district commanders but as staff officers. Did you have a very strong say in who was going to fill what jobs? Do you have the ultimate say?

Admiral O'Neill: Yes, the top jobs, yes. The skipper of a ship, no. Unless there was some doubt in somebody's mind, and the chief officer in personnel would come up with it, but that would happen very, very rarely that I would get into that.

As far as the staff at headquarters was concerned, like the chief of staff, planning and control, and things like that, usually that was left to the Assistant Commandant. He would come in and say, "I'd like to transfer this fellow to a ship to get some sea duty, and bring this other fellow from a ship in here to get some experience in headquarters." That was all right with me. No district commander was ever appointed unless I gave the final word on it.

Peter Spectre: Did you say, "I want him," or did somebody present you a list of choices for recommendation?

Admiral O'Neill: Sometimes it worked that way, and sometimes I would say, "I want this fellow here transferred out here as district commander."

What I would sometimes do, knowing that I wanted that particular man, I would contact him first. Being a friend, I'd say, "How would you like to go to San Francisco as head of the district?"

He'd say, "Fine, tell the personnel officer to put the orders through.

Once you start that, transferring them, then you set up a chain. You get all these things, so then you've got a fight. Maybe you might have 10 or 12 names on it, all these transfers. Then you've got to give that a little thought: "Now, if we transfer this fellow here, how are we going to make out when we come down to the end of the slate here? What's going to happen?" Then it gets a little more complicated. Sometimes it's very simple. Transfer one man to the job and another man to another job, and that ends it.

Peter Spectre: What about the selection of new admirals? How is that selection process?

Admiral O'Neill: By selection board.

Peter Spectre: Did you have any part to play in that?

Admiral O'Neill: No, none whatsoever. I was accused of it in a few cases. The selection board was appointed by the Commandant. He would give them a list of names: "Go down this far. Pick three admirals from this group." Then, after the board met, they would submit those three names to the Commandant. The final analysis was left in the hands of the Secretary of the Treasury. Of course, he depended on the Commandant. If the Commandant approved the three, he would send it over to the Secretary of the Treasury, he would okay it, and then it would go to the White House. From the White House it would go to the Senate for confirmation.

Peter Spectre: Did you ever disapprove one?

Admiral O'Neill: No. You'd have to have a great deal of information to be able to disapprove the appointment of a senior officer, unless you had good and sufficient reasons for it to convince the Secretary. I don't know whether Commandants since my time have disapproved it or not, or how they work it, but I never disapproved it.

Very often I had the feeling that they passed over a better man to come down and pick this man, but I couldn't make an issue of it, because here were five or seven officers sitting there going over the records. The reputation of these officers—they probably felt that they were doing the right thing and had picked the best man in their own minds.

Peter Spectre: It would also be hard for you to say something about that anyway, because they passed over many men to get to you too.

Admiral O'Neill: That's right, a great many officers who had been senior to me all during my period. One of them had been my instructor at the Coast Guard Academy when I was a cadet. He was a lieutenant, and I was a cadet. At that time he was superintendent of the Coast Guard Academy, Admiral Derby.[*]

Peter Spectre: You could influence selections to a certain extent, couldn't you, by the people that you appointed to the board?

Admiral O'Neill: No, there was no way that you could influence the board.

Peter Spectre: You know the people that are going to be on the board, so that they would tend to agree with you. For instance, you wouldn't appoint somebody to the board who was a dissident aviator from back in your past. So you do have a certain amount of influence, sort of a vaguely indirect influence but not to the sense that you can dictate who is going to be selected.

---

[*] Rear Admiral Wilfred N. Derby, USCG, served as Superintendent of the Coast Guard Academy from August 1947 to August 1950. He was in the Coast Guard Academy class of 1911, ten years prior to O'Neill's graduation.

Admiral O'Neill: I always made it perfectly clear in the selection boards in writing that it was entirely in their hands. The Commandant had no part in it whatsoever except to approve or disapprove their selections transmitted to the Secretary of the Treasury. They had a free hand. Who voted for whom was never revealed. If there were five officers on it, maybe three would vote for the man and two against him. I wouldn't know who the three were or who the two were, and I never inquired. I never wanted it to be that way. But it was felt by a few in the service who were passed over that the Commandant did have some influence over the board. There weren't too many cases of that kind that came to my attention. That never presented a problem while I was there.

Peter Spectre: One thing that we've talked around—there isn't much more to talk about, but we haven't touched on the Korean War and the Coast Guard in the Korean War. The Coast Guard wasn't really in the Korean War. Is there any particular reason why not?

Admiral O'Neill: The wars that the Coast Guard has taken part in—we transferred to the Navy if there's a formal declaration of war, or if the President signs a transfer order. Nothing like that happened in the Korean War; we played no part whatsoever.

Peter Spectre: Did you have any desire?

Admiral O'Neill: During that time it was very indirect. We set up a very tight inshore patrol for the harbors. We had plenty of problems of our own in those days to keep body and soul together. That was strictly an Army and Marine Corps operation in Korea. The Navy, of course, was involved, too, on the landings and shore bombardments and plane activity and things like that. But there was nothing involving the Coast Guard.

Peter Spectre: Was there any of what's now called "a hawk and a dove" in the Coast Guard? Were there people that wanted the Coast Guard to become somehow involved, more or less because there was a war being fought, and after all the Coast Guard is a military service, so shouldn't the Coast Guard in some way participate?

Admiral O'Neill: No, there was never any feeling like that of mine or anyone that I knew. That could have happened in the case of some of the officers, maybe the junior officers, but I never heard of it. We had plenty to do without getting involved in a Korean War.

Peter Spectre: You mentioned just briefly the port security question during the Korean War. Was that a very large outfit?

Admiral O'Neill: No. We built a sizable number of these 40-foot inshore patrol boats and 82-footers for surveillance of ships and contacts.

At that time someone got the idea that some Russian ship, or a ship of a satellite country, might smuggle an atomic bomb into New York Harbor or Baltimore or someplace like that, but it never amounted to anything. The inshore patrol had orders then that if a satellite ship came into port, it would be diverted to a port up in Maine, where it would have to be unloaded and searched there. But nothing like that ever happened to my knowledge. Russian ships never came, and the few satellite ships that came in hadn't touched at a Russian port. That was much ado about nothing at that time.

These 40-foot patrol boats are still active in harbors and rivers, and we have them here in the Chesapeake Bay. The 82-footers are more or less on search and rescue work; they're very active in that respect. So the boats came in very handy for that kind of work.

Peter Spectre: I've been working on a manuscript about the history of "the rise and fall of the three-mile limit" as defining the limit of territorial waters. I know that a lot of the Coast Guard's work depends upon this definition of the limits of the territorial waters, for smuggling, for instance, and port security work and national defense.

Right after the Second World War there was a lot of redefinition of the limit of the territorial waters. Lots of countries changed from three miles to 12 miles. In the South American countries—Chile, Ecuador, and Peru—they went to 200 miles. Was the Coast Guard involved in any way in determining territorial waters?

Admiral O'Neill: I don't recall it.

Peter Spectre: Later on, in 1960, the conference about safety at sea, the Coast Guard was involved in that.

In your period of time as Commandant, do you have anything that you're particularly proud of as you look back—something that you did that you look back on and say, "This was really something"?

Admiral O'Neill: No. It was a great honor to be Commandant. I think most commissioned officers have maybe a little secret hope that someday they might become Commandant. A few succeed and a few don't, but it's only one spot and a great many aspirants to the throne.

I enjoyed my service as Commandant. I'm glad to see today that the Coast Guard is growing, is expanding and going ahead. A service has to go ahead or go back; you can't stand still. I'm still very proud of the way the Coast Guard is functioning, and it's in very able hands.

Peter Spectre: You mentioned before we turned the tape machine on, when you retired, or just before you were going to retire, you were asked to stay on for a short period of time.

Admiral O'Neill: Yes, I consulted the Assistant Secretary of the Treasury about a couple of months before my time was up; that was December 31, 1953. I told him that would be the end of my tour of duty, and I would request retirement. I thought four years as Commandant were sufficient. I don't think any officer should serve more than four years. I think that's enough. I felt that way about it and still do.

At that time we were having a little financial difficulty, primarily with the budget section of the Treasury Department, on account of the cuts in the ocean station program. The budget director, or somebody in the Treasury Department, if they had to cut down on some function in the Treasury Department, would pick on the Coast Guard. I said that, and felt like it then, and still do. We were the scapegoat more often than we should have been. That was pretty well known around Washington.

Apparently the Secretary got the idea that if I did retire right then, it would indicate my disagreement with the Treasury policy and the Republican Administration that was handling the Treasury Department. He practically said so, not in those same words, but he told me that the Secretary thought it would be best if I stayed on for another four or five months until all the budget hearings had been finished.

The budget hearings usually started in January on the Hill, and they lasted probably off and on up into March, through the House first and then the Senate. So I said yes, I would stay on for a few more months. But a Commandant can't be appointed for four months, so I was appointed for a full term, and everybody thought that I was going to serve another four years.

Then, all of a sudden, in May it was announced that I was retiring, and Admiral Richmond was the new Commandant. A lot of people said, "Why?"

I told them why; I didn't go into all the details. I said that the Secretary of the Treasury asked me to serve a few more months, and I told him I would. Those were the facts and figures.

Peter Spectre: I always thought that it was a rule that you could only serve four years. It isn't a rule then? You can serve another four years?

Admiral O'Neill: Yes, Admiral Richmond served eight years. Admiral Waesche, during World War II, served I think eight years.[*] Richmond is the only one who has served eight years since Admiral Waesche's day. Farley was four years; I was four years and five months; Richmond was eight years; Roland was four years; and Smith was four years.

Peter Spectre: The person who wanted to serve eight years could serve eight years. Do you think that that's possible?

---

[*] Admiral Waesche's tenure was from June 1936 to December 1945.

Admiral O'Neill: It's possible, yes.

Peter Spectre: In other words, you would say to the Secretary, "I would like to serve four more years." Do you think you could have served four more years?

Admiral O'Neill: I could have served four more years, yes.

Peter Spectre: Why did you feel that four years was enough?

Admiral O'Neill: It's a terrific strain, to begin with. You're harassed in many ways. You're in the old Washington merry-go-round and treadmill. It's a physical strain; it was in those days. I don't know now. Maybe the present and the last few Commandants it didn't bother them at all.

It bothered me because of the problems you face. You wake up at night and think about it. I always tried not to bring my office problems home with me, but you couldn't get away from the fact that you would wake up at 2:00 or 3:00 o'clock in the morning with some kind of a problem, and you'd lie awake for two or three hours trying to solve the problem. That takes a toll, a physical toll. It did for me, and I'm sure it did of others.

I think Admiral Smith, to use the famous expression, took a beating while he was Commandant.[*] I don't know about Roland and the others; I can't answer for them.[†] I know very well—maybe you've heard some of it too—Smith got into difficulties about this selecting reserves. That's just one problem, and I think it aged him a little bit too.

Also, I think it's good to give other officers a chance for the top rank. This old saying that it takes four years to really learn all these problems, and then the next four years he can do a much better job, is a lot of malarkey.

To repeat—I was greatly honored.

---

[*] Admiral Willard J. Smith, USCG, served as Commandant of the Coast Guard from 1 June 1966 to 31 May 1970. His oral history is in the Naval Institute collection.
[†] Admiral Edwin J. Roland, USCG, served as Commandant of the Coast Guard from 1 June 1962 to 1 June 1966. His oral history is in the Naval Institute collection.

Peter Spectre: I really appreciate the time that you've spent with me, and I know something good will come out of it eventually. Thank you very much.

**Index to the Oral History of
Admiral Merlin O'Neill
U.S. Coast Guard (Retired)**

Alaska
 Coast Guard operations in the Bering Sea area in the early 1920s, 13-22
 In 1924 Army fliers had problems in Alaska during an around-the-world flight, 17-18

Alcohol
 In the mid-1920s the Coast Guard patrolled off the East Coast for rumrunners, 25-31, 36-37

Alexander Hamilton, **USCGC**
 Served in the late 1920s as a training ship for Coast Guard Academy cadets, 38, 107

Aleutian Islands
 Coast Guard operations in the Bering Sea area in the early 1920s, 13-22
 In 1924 Army fliers had problems in Alaska during an around-the-world flight, 17-18

Algeria
 In 1943 the attack transport *Leonard Wood* (APA-12) picked up German prisoners at Mers el-Kébir and took them to the United States, 80-81

Algonquin, **USCGC**
 In 1924 operated on Bering Sea Patrol around Alaska, 17-22

Allen, Rear Admiral Edward C., Jr., USCG (USCGA, 1938)
 Served during World War II in the attack transport *Leonard Wood* (APA-12) and in the early 1970s commanded the Fifth Coast Guard District, 79

Amphibious Warfare
 Service of the attack transport *Leonard Wood* (APA-12) in the November 1942 landings in North Africa, 69-75
 Service of the *Leonard Wood* in the July 1943 landings in Sicily, 76-80
 Service of the *Leonard Wood* in the November 1943 landings in the Gilbert Islands, 83-84, 91
 Service of the *Leonard Wood* in the February 1944 landings in the Marshall Islands, 86-87

Apache, **USCGC**
 Cutter that operated out of Baltimore in the mid-1930s, 44-50, 53
 During World War II was used by the Army in the Philippines, 45

Army, U.S.
>Role in connection with the invasion of Sicily in the summer of 1943, 76-80
>Procedures in connection with amphibious operations in World War II, 88-89

Army Air Service, U.S.
>In 1924 Army fliers had problems in Alaska during an around-the-world flight, 17-18

Attu, Aleutian Islands
>Work of the natives in the 1920s, later captured by the Japanese in World War II, 15-16

Baltimore, Maryland
>The Coast Guard cutter *Apache* operated out of Baltimore in the mid-1930s, 44-50
>Coast Guard operations around the port in 1944-45, 52-53, 92-93

Bear, **USCGC**
>Operations around Alaska in the early 1920s, 13

Bender, Admiral Chester R., USCG (USCGA, 1936)
>In the late 1940s was the pilot for the Commandant, Admiral Joseph Farley, and in 1970 became Commandant himself, 98-99, 109-110, 128

Budgetary Issues
>Annual process in the late 1940s-early 1950s in getting Coast Guard budgets approved, 100-104, 114-115, 119-120, 136-137

Caliendo, Captain Anthony J., USCG (Ret.)
>Early in his career, around 1940, had a role in the formation of what became the Coast Guard Auxiliary, 62

Casablanca, French Morocco
>Site of amphibious landings in November 1942, 73-74

Cassin, **USCGC (CG-1)**
>Destroyer that operated off the East Coast in the late 1920s, 36-37

Chesapeake Bay
>A hurricane in the autumn of 1933 caused considerable damage in the Chesapeake Bay area, 44-46
>Operations out of Baltimore by the cutter *Apache* in the mid-1930s, 44-50
>In 1942-43 the attack transport *Leonard Wood* (APA-12) did rehearsals around Cove Point for the invasions of North Africa and Sicily, 67, 69-71, 74-76

Coast Guard, U.S.
Operations in Louisiana in the early years of the 20th century, 2
Operations along the Atlantic Coast in the early 1920s, 8-10, 12, 23-24
Operations along the Pacific Coast in the early 1920s, 11-21
In the mid-1920s patrolled off the Atlantic Coast for rumrunners, 25-31, 36-37
Operations around the Chesapeake Bay are in the mid-1930s, 44-53
Role of Coast Guard Headquarters in the late 1930s-early 1940s, 53-65
In the late 1930s set up the civilian Coast Guard Reserve, which later became the Coast Guard Auxiliary, 55-65
In 1941 the Coast Guard transferred from Treasury to the Navy Department, 32-33, 60-61
A Coast Guard crew manned the Navy attack transport *Leonard Wood* (APA-12) from 1942 to 1944, 66-91
Role of Coast Guard Headquarters in the late 1940s-early 1950s, 97-138
The marine inspection function moved into the Coast Guard in 1942, 116-118
Ocean station role in the 1950s, 120-122
In the 1950s the Coast Guard took over some ships from the Navy, 120-121
Questions over the years as to which cabinet department was the best fit for the service, 32-33, 102-103, 123
Work of Coast Guard promotion boards in the early 1950s, 132-134
Limited role for the service during the Korean War, 134-135

Coast Guard Academy, New London, Connecticut
In 1918-21 was a small school with limited faculty and student body, 4-8
Role of training ships, 1918-21, 7-8
Role of the alumni association, 34
Moved to its current location in 1932, 37
Training and education of cadets in the late 1920s and early 1930s, 38-43
In the late 1940s-early 1950s President Harry S. Truman made a visit to the Coast Guard Academy, 104-105
In 1946 acquired the bark *Eagle* (WIX-327) as a sail training ship, 105-107

Coast Guard Auxiliary
Civilian organization that began as the Coast Guard Reserve in the late 1930s and was later renamed, 55-65

Coast Guard Reserve, U.S.
A temporary uniformed reserve was established around the beginning of World War II, 63-65
Operation of shortly after the end of World War II, 114-115, 118-119

Commercial Ships
Operations off the Pacific Coast in the early 1920s, 14, 16, 19-20
A banana-laden ship ran aground in the Chesapeake Bay in the mid-1930s, 48

Congress, U.S.
    Role in establishing the civilian Coast Guard Reserve in the late 1930s, 57
    Process in the late 1940s-early 1950s in getting annual Coast Guard budgets approved, 100-101, 114-115, 119-120, 136-137

Demobilization
    Thousands of men and women left the Coast Guard when World War II ended, 99-100, 114-116

Derby, Rear Admiral Wilfred N., USCG (USCGA, 1911)
    Served as Superintendent of the Coast Guard Academy from August 1947 to August 1950, 133

Dimick, Professor Chester E.
    Taught mathematics at the Coast Guard Academy in the 1920s and 1930s, 6, 39, 41

Eagle, **USCGC (WIX-327)**
    In 1946 began serving as a sail training ship at the Coast Guard Academy, 105-107

Eisenhower, President Dwight D.
    In 1953-54, early in his administration, there were questions about the best department for the Coast Guard, 33, 102-104, 123

Emmett, Captain Robert R. M., USN (USNA, 1908)
    Used the attack transport *Leonard Wood* (APA-12) as his flagship during World War II amphibious operations, 71, 75, 77

Eniwetok, Marshall Islands
    Invaded by U.S. amphibious forces in February 1944, 86-90

Ericsson **(CG-5), USCGC**
    Former Navy destroyer that the Coast Guard used in the mid-1920s to patrol for rumrunners, 25-31, 34-36

Farley, Admiral Joseph F., USCG (USCGA, 1912)
    As a junior officer served in the cutter *Gresham* in the early 1920s, 50-51
    Was executive officer of the cutter *Mojave* in 1924, 51
    From 1946 to 1949 served as Commandant of the Coast Guard, 50, 96-98, 105, 107-110

Fifth Coast Guard District, Norfolk, Virginia
    Operations in the district in 1945, as World War II was winding down, involved ties with the Navy, 95-96

Fishing
    In the Alaska area in the early 1920s, 16-17

Food
    On board the Coast Guard cutter *Haida* (WPG-45) in the early 1920s, 16-17
    A banana-laden ship ran aground in the Chesapeake Bay in the mid-1930s, 48

German Army
    In 1943 the attack transport *Leonard Wood* (APA-12) took a number of captured German soldiers from Algeria to the United States, 80-82

Gilbert Islands
    Role of the attack transport *Leonard Wood* (APA-12) during the U.S. invasion of Makin in November 1943, 83-85, 91

Gresham, **USCGC**
    Operations out of New York in the early 1920s, 8-10, 12, 23-24, 51

Gunnery – Naval
    In connection with the amphibious landings at French Morocco in November 1942, 73-74
    Support of the amphibious landings in the Marshall Islands in February 1944, 87

Haida, **USCGC (WPG-45)**
    Operations out of Seattle in the early 1920s extended as far north as the Bering Sea, 11-19

Hawaii
    In 1943 the attack transport *Leonard Wood* (APA-12) staged through Hawaii en route to invasions in the Gilbert and Marshall islands, 83

Humphrey, George M.
    As Secretary of the Treasury in the mid-1950s questioned whether the Coast Guard should be in the Treasury Department, 32-33, 102-104
    In 1953-54 extended O'Neill's term as Commandant of the Coast Guard, 136-137

Icebreaking
    By the Coast Guard cutter *Apache* in 1934 in the Chesapeake Bay, 47-49

Itasca, **USCGC**
    Used around 1920 as a Coast Guard Academy training ship, 7

Japanese Navy
    Reaction to the U.S. landings in the Gilberts and Marshalls in 1943-44, 85-88

Jenkins, Lieutenant Commander William A., USCG (USCGA, 1942)
    In the early 1950s served as aide and pilot for the Coast Guard Commandant, 110

Kennedy, President John F.
In the early 1960s was impressed by the appearance of the Coast Guard bark *Eagle* (WIX-327), 106

Korean War
Limited role for the Coast Guard during the war, 134-135

***Leonard Wood*, USS (AP-25/APA-12)**
In 1942 was converted from a straight troop transport to an amphibious attack transport, 66
Characteristics of the ship, 67-68
Service in the November 1942 landings in North Africa, 69-75
Service in the July 1943 landings in Sicily, 76-80
Service in the November 1943 landings on Makin in the Gilbert Islands, 83-85, 91
Service in February 1944 landings in the Marshall Islands, 86-90
Shipyard overhaul in California in early 1944, 90

Lighthouses
In 1939 the Bureau of Lighthouses moved from the Commerce Department to become part of the Coast Guard, 111-112, 116-118

***Liscome Bay*, USS (CVE-56)**
Torpedoed and sunk by a Japanese submarine in the Gilbert Islands in November 1943, 85

Makin, Gilbert Islands
Role of the attack transport *Leonard Wood* (APA-12) during the U.S. invasion in November 1943, 83-85

Marine Corps, U.S.
Invasion of the Marshall Islands in February 1944, 86-87, 90
Training of beach parties in 1944 at the Quantico, Virginia, Marine Corps base, 91-92

Marion Military Institute, Marion, Alabama
In 1918 served as a prep school for prospective service academy students, 3-4

Marshall Islands
Role of the attack transport *Leonard Wood* (APA-12) during the U.S. invasion of Kwajalein and Eniwetok in February 1944, 86-90

Martin, Major Frederick L., U.S. Army Air Service
Problems in Alaska during an around-the-world flight in 1924, 18

Mers el-Kébir, Algeria
    In 1943 the attack transport *Leonard Wood* (APA-12) took a number of captured German soldiers from this port to the United States, 80-82

Military Academy, U.S., West Point, New York
    Regimen for cadets in 1917-18, 2-4, 41

Mojave, **USCGC**
    Transfer via Panama from the Pacific to the Atlantic in late 1924, 22-23, 51

Morocco, French
    Service of the attack transport *Leonard Wood* (APA-12) in the November 1942 landings in North Africa, 69-75

Norfolk, Virginia
    Difficulties between civilians and service families during World War II, 94-95

North Africa
    Service of the attack transport *Leonard Wood* (APA-12) in the November 1942 landings in French Morocco, 69-75

Olsen, Rear Admiral Carl B., USCG (USCGA, 1928)
    Was selected for flag rank in the 1950s after dropping his aviator qualification, 128

O'Neill, Admiral Merlin, USCG (Ret.) (USCGA, 1921)
    Parents of, 1, 4
    Wife Esther, 10-11, 24, 37, 44, 53, 65, 91-92, 94, 97
    Daughters Patricia and Marilyn, 44, 53, 91-92, 109
    Boyhood in Ohio and Louisiana in the early years of the 20th century, 1-2
    In 1917-18 as a cadet at West Point, 2-4, 41
    Was a student at Marion Military Institute in 1918, 3-4
    As a cadet from 1918 to 1921 at the Coast Guard Academy, 4-8, 11-12, 32
    In 1921-22 served in the cutter *Gresham*, 8-10, 12, 23-24, 50-51
    In 1922-23 served in the cutter *Haida* (WPG-45), 11, 13-16
    In 1924 served in the cutter *Algonquin*, 17-22
    Brief service in the cutter *Mojave* in 1924, 22-23, 51
    In 1925-27 served as executive officer and later commanding officer of the destroyer *Ericsson* (CG-5), 25-31, 34-36
    Served on the staff of the Coast Guard Academy from 1927 to 1930, 37-43
    Brief duty in other destroyers in the early 1930s, 36-37
    Commanded the cutter *Apache*, 1933-35, 44-50
    Served in Coast Guard Headquarters in Washington from 1935 to 1942, 52-65
    Commanded the Navy attack transport *Leonard Wood* (APA-12) from 1942 to 1944, 66-91
    Brief duty in 1944 at the Quantico, Virginia, Marine Corps base, 91-92

In 1944 headed the Baltimore subsection of the Fifth Coast Guard District, 52-53, 92-93
In 1945 commanded the Fifth Coast Guard District in Norfolk, 93-96, 130-131
Served 1946-49 as Assistant Commandant of the Coast Guard, 97-115
Selection in 1949 to become the next Commandant, 107-109
Served 1950-54 as Commandant of the Coast Guard, 102-103, 122-138

Penn, Commander Richard T., Jr., USCG (USCGA, 1949)
Coast Guard officer who married Admiral O'Neill's daughter Patricia, 109

Philadelphia Navy Yard
In the mid-1920s reactivated destroyers for use by the Coast Guard to patrol for rumrunners, 25-26

Phillips, Captain Wallace B., USN (USNA, 1911)
Used the attack transport *Leonard Wood* (APA-12) as his flagship during World War II amphibious operations, 77

Power Squadron, U.S.
In the late 1930s was concerned about the establishment of a civilian Coast Guard Reserve, 58-59

Prisoners of War
In 1943 the attack transport *Leonard Wood* (APA-12) took a number of captured German soldiers from Algeria to the United States, 80-82

Prohibition
In the mid-1920s the Coast Guard patrolled off the East Coast for rumrunners, 25-31

Quantico, Virginia
Training of beach parties in 1944 at this Marine Corps base, 91-92

Richmond, Admiral Alfred C., USCG (USCGA, 1925)
Served as Coast Guard Assistant Commandant, 1950-54, and Commandant, 1954-62, 102, 110-111, 123-124, 128, 137

Rose, H. Chapman
Served 1953-55 as Assistant Secretary of the Treasury, 103-104

Sailing
Sail training at the Coast Guard Academy around 1920, 7
In 1946 the bark *Eagle* (WIX-327) began serving as a sail training ship at the Coast Guard Academy, 105-107

Search and Rescue
By the Coast Guard cutter *Apache* in the mid-1930s in the Chesapeake Bay, 44-48

Selection Boards
   Work of Coast Guard promotion boards in the early 1950s, 132-134

***Shaw*, USCGC (CG-22)**
   Served in the late 1920s as a training ship for Coast Guard Academy cadets, 38-39

Ship Handling
   In Coast Guard destroyers in the mid-1920s, 27-28

Sicily
   Role of the attack transport *Leonard Wood* (APA-12) in connection with the invasion of Sicily in the summer of 1943, 76-80

Smith, Admiral Willard J., USCG (USCGA, 1933)
   Served as Commandant of the Coast Guard, 1966-70, 137-138

Snyder, John W.
   As Secretary of the Treasury, 1946-53, the Coast Guard came under his purview, 104-105, 107-108, 110

Training
   On board the attack transport *Leonard Wood* (APA-12) in 1942, 69-70
   Of beach parties in 1944 at the Quantico, Virginia, Marine Corps base, 91-92

Treasury Department
   In 1941 the Coast Guard transferred from Treasury to the Navy Department, 32-33, 60-61
   Process in the late 1940s-early 1950s in getting the Coast Guard's annual budgets approved, 101-104, 119-120, 136-137
   In 1953-54, early in the administration of President Dwight Eisenhower, there were questions about whether Treasury was the best department for the Coast Guard, 33, 102-104, 123

Truman, President Harry S.
   In the late 1940s-early 1950s made a visit to the Coast Guard Academy, 104-105

Waesche, Admiral Russell R., USCG (USCGA, 1906)
   Served from 1936 to 1945 as Coast Guard Commandant, 51-52, 55-57, 59, 64-65, 96-97, 137

Weather
   A hurricane in the autumn of 1933 caused considerable damage in the Chesapeake Bay area, 44-46